SHORT SELLING YOUR HOME

HOMEOWNER'S GUIDE :

How To Navigate and Benefit from Today's Real Estate Market Crisis

By

Ronald O. Escobar, MBA

and
Tim And Julie Harris

Preface by Ron Escobar

In these tough economic times is easy to give in to the stress associated with "losing one's home". We very often think that our home is our castle, or it is where we are protected and offer protection to our loved ones from the "outside world". We usually associate the physical structure, or house with "our home". I submit that in the times where the economy and market has been turned upside-down, we have to respond and adjust accordingly, and **change our underlying assumptions**...

In my personal experience I found the old adage *"Home is Where your Heart Is"* very much alive. You don't need that over-priced home and high mortgage to provide security, shelter and love to yourself and those around you... you can do the same in the house across the street at a price that will not break your budget and make economic sense.

In my experience, the sooner you realize these changes and adjust your paradigm, the sooner you will be able to move forward and forget about all that stress associated with an unaffordable mortgage. Let the bank deal with the loss of value! You focus on you and not a building.

You can be in control of your destiny. Do not let your attachment to a building dictate your happiness. Read the following pages and learn about your options and focus on things you can control and experience your happiness now, and not tomorrow.

Table Of Contents

Chapter One.

A National Epidemic Is Looming. Are You Ready?

Chapter Two.

How Bad Is It?

Chapter Three.

Ok, I Get It. A Short Sale May Be My Best Option. Tell Me More.

Chapter Four.

What Is A Mortgage Foreclosure?

Chapter Five.

You Have Been Warned: Foreclosure Scams.

Chapter Six.

What Are The Options For Homeowners In Foreclosure?

Chapter Seven.

You Now Want To Short Sale Your Home: Top 10 Short Sale Questions, Answered.

Chapter Eight.
I Thought Rates Were Falling. Won't That Help?

Chapter Nine.
Life After Short Sale..When You Want To Buy A Home Again…FHA To The Rescue.

Chapter Ten.
Something You Should Know: The Death Of The Home Equity Loan - Millions Of Homeowners Shut Out.

Chapter One

A National Epidemic Is Looming. Are You Ready?

Are you stressed out about mortgage payments? Do you think your only option is a foreclosure? Is a short sale right for you? Millions and millions of homeowners are asking themselves the same questions. It is projected that over 20,000,000 homeowners will have negative equity in their homes in the very near future. In other words, they will owe more on their homes than they are worth. Over 2.9 million homes have foreclosed in the last three years and the number is only expected to grow. Expect the effects of the estate recession to ripple for years to come.

What can you do now?

There is expected to be massive tsunami of homeowners who are simply making the decision to sell their homes through a short sale vs. staying in a home, hoping that one day it may be worth what they paid.

No one is safe. News stories from across the country tell the tales of both celebrities and average Americans who are all considering selling their homes through a short sale.

Selling your home through a short sale doesn't need to be a shameful, life-ruining experience. Sometimes short selling your mortgage simply **makes smart**

economic sense, especially for homeowners who find themselves "upside down" — that is, they owe more on their mortgage than their house is worth.

Late last year, CNBC Financial Guru Jim Cramer was telling homeowners to 'Just Walk Away'. (Watch the video on YouTube.com.)

We are clearly in uncharted waters. The current housing crisis is different from all the previous housing recessions. It is well known that many financial institutions sold mortgages in a deceptive manner — for example, by approving people for loans they couldn't really afford — then why should homeowners feel obliged to honor their commitments?

From a homeowner's perspective, why should they stay in a home that is depreciating? Often times it's possible to rent the same style home in the same area for half (or less) than their current mortgage payment. Assuming it takes years for the market to recover, the homeowner who sells their home via a short sale now will be far ahead of the person who 'stuck it out'.

Here is an example:

Starting May of 2008:

* Homeowner paid $500,000 at the market peak in late 2006. Homeowner put down 5% and did a 7 year interest only mortgage. Monthly payment including principle, interest, taxes and insurance is $4200 per month.

* Assuming the property has depreciated 30% and is now worth only $350,000, the owner has negative equity or is 'upside down' by $150,000.

* The market is continuing to depreciate and is projected to level off in mid to late 2011. In other words, months and months of more losses for the homeowner. -but who knows how long this economic times will actually last.

Option 1
Homeowner can 'stick it out' and keep the home. They will continue to make their monthly interest only payment/ house upkeep of $4200 per month. They will pay $50,400 per year to keep the home. They are deeply 'upside down' in the home with massive negative equity. By late 2011, maybe -that is a big maybe, the home's value has stopped depreciating.

The market stays flat for at least a year thereafter. The inventory levels have to sell off. In late 2012 or early 2013 the market then starts to slowly appreciate again. Best case the home starts to appreciate at 5% per year. Based on this rough example it will take at least 9 to10 years for that home to be worth what that owner paid in 2006. During that time the homeowner will have paid $50,400 per year. Do the math. That's $352,800 spent to stay in the home and 'stick it out'.

Option 2

Homeowner lists the home with an agent trained in doing short sales. The home sells and the bank agrees to accept the loss in equity as the short sale. Bank loses $150,000. Homeowner moves to a rental home in the same neighborhood and pays rent of $2000 per month. Half of his previous house payment. Homeowner saves the difference between what he had been paying for the owned home and his new rent payment. $26,400 per year. Yes, the homeowner does have significant negative credit ramifications as a result of their short sale. This negative credit will prevent them from buying a home for the next 18-24 months. With this option he can sit out the real estate recession and jump back in when the market has hit bottom. If he times it right he can buy at the markets bottom. This time he will have a more significant down payment and a better quality mortgage.

Let's be very clear about this next point...Yes, there is damage to your credit. According to national experts, after a short sale, a person's credit will go down by 300 + or - points and then prevent them from buying using a government backed mortgage for up to 24 months. With a *foreclosure*, the credit is damaged for up to 4 years preventing someone from obtaining a government-backed mortgage.

Many home owners who are now short selling their properties are going to want to buy houses again someday; and when they do, lenders are going to want to make money lending them money to do so.

Option 3:
Loan programs are constantly changing, and now days it is possible to simultaneously short-sale a property while "downgrading" and buying another property. This means you can short sale your home, and buy the home next block which is now cheaper and technically a downgrade from your current home. you will then have the same standard of living and a much lower payment.

Chapter Two

How Bad Is It?

One thing is certain: Foreclosures are on the rise. Cities in California, Ohio, Florida and Michigan just posted the highest foreclosure rates in the U.S., according to RealtyTrac, a private firm.

RealtyTrac is the go-to source for the best foreclosure information. This information is from a recent report that they released. If you want to obtain current, up to the minute information on foreclosures in your area go to their website. www.realtytrac.com

Foreclosure Activity Up 112 Percent From Q1 2007 California and Florida Cities Accounts for 13 of Top 20 Metro Areas -

"RealtyTrac, the leading online marketplace for foreclosure properties, released its Q1 2008 U.S. Foreclosure Market Report™, which shows foreclosure filings — default notices, auction sale notices and bank repossessions — were reported on 649,917 properties during the first quarter, a 23 percent increase from the previous quarter and a 112 percent increase from the first quarter of 2007. The report also shows that one in every 194 U.S. households received a foreclosure filing during the first quarter. Foreclosure activity in the first quarter increased on a year-over-year basis in 46 out of the 50 states and in 90 of the nation's 100 largest metro

areas, demonstrating that most regions of the country are seeing more foreclosures."

Nevada, California, Arizona have the highest state foreclosure rates. One in every 54 Nevada households received a foreclosure filing during the first quarter, the highest foreclosure rate among the states and 3.6 times the national average. Foreclosure filings were reported on 19,595 Nevada properties during the quarter, up 3 percent from the previous quarter and up 137 percent from the first quarter of 2007.

Foreclosure filings were reported on 169,831 California properties during the first quarter, the highest total among the states and a rate of one in every 78 households — the nation's second highest foreclosure rate. Foreclosure activity in California increased 32 percent from the previous quarter and was up nearly 213 percent from the first quarter of 2007, and much higher in 2009 and 2010.

Arizona documented the nation's third highest state foreclosure rate, with one in every 95 households receiving a foreclosure filing during the quarter. Foreclosure filings were reported on 27,404 Arizona properties during the quarter, up 45 percent from the previous quarter and up nearly 245 percent from the first quarter of 2007, and much higher in 2009 and 2010.

Foreclosure filings were reported on 87,893 Florida properties during the first quarter, the second highest state total and giving Florida the nation's fourth highest foreclosure rate — one in every 97 households received a foreclosure filing during the quarter. Foreclosure activity in the state was up 17 percent from the previous quarter and up 178 percent from the first quarter of 2007.

Colorado foreclosure activity increased 33 percent from the previous quarter and 78 percent from the first quarter of 2007, and the state's foreclosure rate ranked No. 5 among the states. Foreclosure filings were reported on 18,996 Colorado properties during the quarter, a rate of one in every 110 households.

Other states with foreclosure rates among the top 10 were Georgia, Michigan, Ohio, Massachusetts and Connecticut.

The Q1 2008 U.S. Foreclosure Market Report also ranks the nation's 100 largest metropolitan areas by foreclosure rate. California and Florida metro areas accounted for 13 of the top 20 metro foreclosure rates, with the California cities of Stockton and Riverside-San Bernardino taking the No. 1 and No. 2 spots.

One in every 30 Stockton households received a foreclosure filing during the quarter — 6.6 times the national average — and one in every 38 Riverside-San Bernardino households received a foreclosure filing during the quarter — more than five times the national average. Other California metro areas in the top 20 included Bakersfield at No. 4, Sacramento at

No. 5, San Diego at No. 9, Oakland at No. 10, Fresno at No. 12, Los Angeles at No. 17 and Orange County at No. 19.

Las Vegas documented the third highest metro foreclosure rate, with one in every 44 households receiving a foreclosure filing during the quarter. The metro area's foreclosure activity increased 1 percent from the previous quarter and 134 percent from the first quarter of 2007.

Detroit foreclosure activity in the first quarter decreased 22 percent from the previous quarter and was down almost 4 percent from the first quarter of 2007, but the metro area's foreclosure rate still ranked No. 6, with one in every 68 households receiving a foreclosure filing during the quarter. Phoenix foreclosure activity increased 46 percent from the previous quarter and 294 percent from the first quarter of 2007, and the metro area's foreclosure rate ranked No. 7, with one in every 70 households receiving a foreclosure filing during the quarter.

The highest ranked Florida metro area was Fort Lauderdale, which ranked No. 8 with one in every 73 households receiving a foreclosure filing during the quarter. Other Florida metro areas in the top 20 included Orlando at No. 13, Miami at No. 14 and Sarasota-Bradenton-Venice at No. 15. The foreclosure rate in Tampa-St. Petersburg-Clearwater ranked No. 21.

Chapter Three

Ok, I Get It…A Short Sale May Be My Best Option…Tell Me More…

A short sale is when a lender accepts a discount on a mortgage to avoid a possible foreclosure auction or bankruptcy. For example: A homeowner, who is facing foreclosure, has an existing first mortgage of $500,000. The market value of the home is $350,000. Long story short, the lender accepts the offer for $350,000 and the home is sold.

That's a short sale.

Why are lenders so eager to take such a huge discount? Banks do not like bad loans. If they see an opportunity where they can sell the property without the huge loss of a foreclosure, they will do it. Some lenders report that if the home goes into foreclosure by the time the home actually closes with the new buyer, the lender will be lucky to net 50% of the original loan balance.

Bottom line from the lenders perspective? They are in the business of lending money, not owning homes. If they can accept a short sale offer and rid themselves of the bad loan AND net more, vs the home going into foreclosure, they will do it every time. It's simply smart business.

Time is not on your side when you are considering a short sale. You must act quickly and work only with a seasoned real estate expert who has successfully completed and graduated from advanced real estate education programs like Harris Real Estate University.

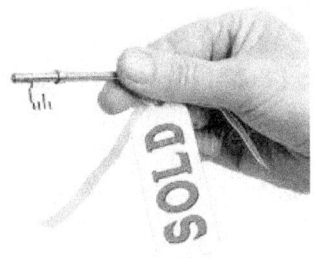

YOU AVOID A FORECLOSURE ON YOUR CREDIT

YOU STAY IN CONTROL

YOU HAVE A WELL THOUGHT OUT TIMELINE

YOU AVOID EVICTION

YOU CAN RECOVER QUICKLY

Chapter Four

What is Mortgage Foreclosure?

Mortgage foreclosure simply means the deed can only be foreclosed through court action. Mortgage foreclosure is usually referred to as a judicial foreclosure.

A mortgage is a security document that allows the borrower to keep title of the property while using the property as security or collateral for a loan. The lender then places a lien on the property in the event the owner does not pay the agreed payment. When the borrower pays off the loan, the lender gives the borrower a satisfaction of mortgage that removes the lien from the property. About half the states in the U.S. use mortgage foreclosure as the means of satisfying the loan balance.

As with most mortgage foreclosure lawsuits, it starts with a summons and a complaint is issued to the borrower and any other parties with inferior rights in the property. Usually the lender's attorney is the one who issues the notice. The complaint is usually filed in the court where the trial is to be held. Here's the interesting part. Once the borrower has been notified, he or she has 20 days to respond back to the court challenging them on the mortgage foreclosure lawsuit. Once this occurs, the court now has 40 days to respond back to the borrower. Keep in mind that each correspondence must be legit and deal with some specific part of the complaint. This process may go back and forth as long as the borrower finds something erroneous with the complaint. This slows a mortgage foreclosure greatly because it must go through the court system. It may go as long as a year if needs be or even longer. This is how many homeowners stay in their homes for months often years after they have stopped making their house payments.

THE BANK IS IN CONTROL

THEY ARE QUICK TO EVICT AND SECURE
THE PROPERTY

YOUR CREDIT IS DAMAGED FOR A LONGER TIME

YOU DONT KNOW WHEN IS GOING TO HAPPEN

Chapter Five

You Have Been Warned: Foreclosure Scams on the Rise!

Foreclosure Scams are on the rise because of the increasing number of foreclosures. It's very important as homeowners to know about these scams..

Common Foreclosure Scams

1. EQUITY SKIMMING:
You are approached by a "buyer" that offers to buy your home at full asking price. The potential buyer claims he will solve all your financial problems by "promising" to pay off your mortgage. He claims to take over the existing mortgage and give you a sum of money after the property is sold. But in order to do so, he suggests that you move out right away and deed the property over to him. So you move out and assume the "buyer" will continue to make the mortgage payments. However, the "buyer" collects rent for the next 6 - 8 months and does not make any mortgage payments. The lender has no choice but to foreclose and all the while you have no idea what's happening because you've moved out.

2. THE BAIT-AND-SWITCH:
Very similar to taking over "subject to", but the acclaimed buyer is only after the equity. The buyer tells the homeowners he will bring the mortgage current and tells them they can stay in the home. But in order to do so, he must have a few documents

signed that protect his interest and gives him ownership of the property. Then a few weeks down the road, the homeowner receives an eviction notice.

3. THE BAILOUT:

Again very similar to the previous two, where the homeowners sign over the deed with the assumption that they will be able to remain in the house as a renter or lease it back from the buyer and eventually buy it back over time. The terms of these types of scams are so harsh that they make it nearly impossible to buy-back which was the plan to begin with. The homeowner is left with nothing and the buyer walks off with most or all of the equity.

4. PHANTOM ASSISTANCE:

Typically these are online companies claiming to have the magic touch in stopping the foreclosure auction. They know all the ins and outs and what to say to the lender to stop the auction. Then these companies charge outrageous fees for simple phone calls and paperwork the homeowner could have completed themselves.

5. COUNSELING AGENCIES:

Some groups, most of them online, calling themselves "counseling agencies" may approach you or ask you to submit your information for a personal consultation to review your situation. They then proceed to offer certain services for a fee. Most of the time these "special services" you are paying for are FREE, such as negotiating a new payment plan with your lender, working out a forbearance, or lowering your interest rate. These are all things your lender will assist you with at no charge. Be careful giving ANYONE money online that claims they can assist you out of foreclosure. There are dozens of good, non-profit organizations and free counseling agencies that are ready and willing to assist.

6. Short Sale Companies. This is the newest breed of companies to avoid. Here is the bottom line, they make all their money from the fees you pay them at the start of the process. In other words, they have little to no incentive to get your short sale actually accepted and closed.

NOT A SCAM: One of the largest foreclosure assistance programs right now is 888-995-HOPE. This is available to any homeowner in America having trouble paying their mortgage. It is <u>provided free of charge</u> by the Homeownership Preservation Foundation, a nonprofit dedicated to preserving homeownership.

Here are a few things you can do to avoid foreclosure scams...

* DON'T SIGN any papers that you don't fully understand, or you could make bad matters worse.

* DON'T SIGN any papers that you feel pressured into signing. Take your time.

* DON'T MAKE mortgage payments to anyone other than your lender.

* DON'T SIGN over the deed without some closure or agreement for your protection. Talk to your attorney or title company if you need help.

* DON'T EVER pay anyone who claims to stop foreclosure. You can stop the auction yourself.

What is Short Sale Flopping?

A Short Sale "flopper" works to drive down the price of your home so that your lender will allow you to sell your home for much less than it's worth. In order to pull it off, the Short Sale flopper must find a home appraiser who agrees to be part of the scam. Without this valuable player, the flopper won't be successful at undervaluing your property.

It works like this: once the flopper drives down the price of your home and secures your property in Short Sale, he then finds a buyer (or may already have a naive buyer lined up) who will buy the property for thousands of dollars above the Short Sale price. Then your lender, not the flopper, takes the loss.

And, if you're not protected against being sued by your lender, they can come after you to pay the deficiency left by this "flop." That means that if your Short Sale agreement doesn't protect you from being subjected to your lender's deficiency judgment, you could be responsible for paying thousands of dollars while the buyer walks away with your property. And, believe me, the bank will have the right to chase you for any shortfall.

Chapter Six

**What are the Options For Homeowners Facing
Foreclosure?**

1. Try to "make nice" with your lender. You can call
your lender and ask them to reinstate the loan. You
may be allowed to reinstate or make the loan current
by paying a lump sum or making scheduled payments
to your lender over a given amount of time. Just
explain to them you had a few bad months and things
are now better and most lenders will try to work
something out with you.

2. IF you have equity, refinance. Usually the lender
would refinance the existing loan and include as part
of the new loan any late payments, and fees that you
would need to regain control. It would all be
"wrapped" into one mortgage.

3. Assuming you have no equity and have to sell, you
can list your home with a Realtor who has been
trained how to do short sales. Almost always your
best option.

4. You can give the property back to the lender. If
there are no other liens on the title, the lender may
agree to take the property back. This process of
transferring ownership from you to the lender under
these circumstances is called a Deed in Lieu of
Foreclosure, and is sometimes referred to as a
"friendly foreclosure" because in essence that what it

is. You just walk away. You must discuss this with your lender.

5. You can file bankruptcy. *First, you need to seek the advice of a attorney. In no way are we trying to provide legal advice. Only an attorney can give legal advice.* The two most common "chapters" of bankruptcy are Chapter 7 and Chapter 13. Bankruptcies are "work out" others are "wipe out". Chapter 7 is the "wipe out" and Chapter 13 is the "work out". Bankruptcy is a federal court action designed to help individuals repay their debts or eliminate their debts depending on their circumstances. Chapter 13 bankruptcies are designed to reorganize debts in an effort to repay all debt. Chapter 7 bankruptcies are geared more towards liquidation of assets. Both Chapter 7 and Chapter 13 immediately stop the foreclosure process and any creditors from taking further action against you.

Chapter 7 Bankruptcy

When someone files a Chapter 7 bankruptcy, all assets are frozen. The attorney creates what is called an automatic stay. Meaning everything "Stays" put. The homeowners can't buy anything, they can't sell anything, and they can't even give away anything. If they try to sell their home, they couldn't. If they try to give away money in savings, they can't. Any unsecured debt like credit cards, unsecured loans, etc. are eliminated or wiped out. They do not exist anymore. Then the trustee or attorney who represents the court and the creditors will look at all the assets (house, car, furniture, equipment) anything of value and decide what must be liquidated to pay some of the debt that was wiped out.

If the homeowners are in the middle of foreclosure, a Chapter 7 will stop the foreclosure process. Usually banks will then ask the trustee to release the property from the automatic stay so they may continue with the foreclosure process. Once the property has been released from the bankruptcy, the foreclosure process starts right where it left off. Typically you have anywhere from 3-5 weeks until the foreclosure process begins again.

Chapter 13 Bankruptcy

When someone files a Chapter 13, they don't take all the assets and sell them. Instead they take all the monthly payments and discount them for pennies on the dollar. It's like a debt consolidation plan. Whatever amount is agreed upon has to be paid to the bankruptcy count every month for the next 3-5 years. So the homeowners get to keep their house, their cars, and all their assets. Now, as long as the homeowner stays current with the mortgage payments and pays the amount agreed upon, they will be fine. However, if any payments are missed, the trustee will dismiss the bankruptcy and the foreclosure process will begin again.

6. And finally, you can just let it go to foreclosure. Basically you don't do anything. You leave with nothing in hand and a foreclosure on your credit report. This is without question the worst option of all.

Another solution available is the Soldier Relief Act of 1940. When a property is owned by a person in the military and the mortgage payments are not made, then this relief act may stop foreclosure based on certain criteria. The person has to be in active duty in order to qualify. The mortgage loan had to be established before the soldier was called out to active duty. Not only will this stop foreclosure, but it will stop seizure of any personal property while the soldier is actively serving and several months thereafter.

Chapter Seven

You Now Want To Do A Short Sale. Top 10 Seller Short Sale Questions, Answered.

Number 10

I can't make my house payments but I do have an ability to pay back all or part of the negative equity. Also, I want to preserve my credit score...is a short sale right for me?

Probably not. In cases where the seller can pay back all or part of the negative equity (usually to the 2nd lien holder) it makes sense for them to work out a *repayment plan*. The lender will then release the lien and allow the home to close.

Number 9

If I pay mortgage insurance and default on my loan, wouldn't that cover the deficiency amount?
The mortgage insurance is not there for your protection, it protects the mortgage lender.

Number 8

Do I have to have my home 'Approved' by my lender prior to offering it for sale as a short sale?
No. Technically speaking, there is no such thing as being 'Short Sale Approved'. The actual *approval* only happens with an accepted offer.

Number 7

I just missed a payment and I know I will miss more....how long does the foreclosure process take and is there time to do a short sale?

The foreclosure process takes differing times depending on your state. In the Midwest a foreclosure can take over a year. In California it's taking 6+ months. Generally speaking a well-priced short sale being processed by an *educated short sale listing agent* will sell and close in less than 120 days.

Number 6
Will I still have to pay property taxes if I do a short sale?

Property taxes will always have to be paid as part of any accepted short sale. Whether it's you or the lender depends on their policies and the specific agreement you reach while negotiating the short sale.

Number 5
I owe more than my home is worth and I can't make the payment, do I have to somehow qualify for a short sale?

The simple answer is NO. If someone can't make their payment and they are otherwise insolvent they qualify for a short sale. Note: insolvent simply means their total debts are great than their assets or they cannot make the payment, keep in mind the lender's options are limited... either they accept the short sale or they foreclose and either way they are not getting more than what the home is worth in California.

Number 4

Do I have to pay income taxes? I have heard that I will get a 1099. Will the loss the bank takes be treated as a taxable gain to me..the seller..is this true?! It WAS true, now it's not. Consult your Tax Attorney or Qualified CPA. Very recently the tax law was modified and now most people who do a short sale will have no taxes due.

Number 3

How do you, my listing agent get paid? Who pays your commission?
The bank will pay the commission along with all the other usual closing costs.

Number 2

Do I have to miss a payment to do a Short Sale?
No. Late last year most major lenders started accepting short sale offers from sellers who have never missed a payment.

Number 1

I want to do a short sale and have a 2nd mortgage, does this make me ineligible?

No. Both of your lenders will need to be satisfied in some way to complete the short sale. If your first lender will be paid off by the sale, then you just negotiate the terms with the second lender. Most short sales do involve 1st and 2nd lien holder.

Chapter Eight

But, I Thought Rates Were Falling. Won't That Help Me?

The Federal Reserve has been lowering rates to bail out the economy. Does this mean that mortgage rates will fall?

In some cases yes in most cases no...read on.

Let's start with the 30-year fixed rate mortgage. The 30-year fixed rate mortgage is not tied to short-term treasuries. Fixed mortgage rates are tied to long-term bond yields that move based on the outlook for the economy and inflation. True, even as the Fed has lowered rates, the 30-year fixed has come down, but that's because of the outlook for slower economic growth in the months ahead. While the decline in treasury yields has helped push mortgage rates lower, the decline in long term rates hasn't been in lockstep thanks to the fact that these mortgages are securitized and sold on the global market. Investors now demand a higher risk premium on these mortgages due to higher delinquencies and foreclosures.

Next let's take a look at 7 and 5-1 Adjustable Rate Mortgages (ARMs) Yes, this is good news if your 5-year (or 7 year) ARM is pegged to a treasury index. So if you're facing a reset on, say, a $200,000 loan, you're now getting a payment increase of about $150 a month, as opposed to $370 a month, which you would have had before the Fed started cutting rates.

Do the Fed Rate Drops Help Sub-Prime mortgage Holders?

Nope. Unfortunately if you have a sub-prime ARM it is more than likely pegged to LIBOR, which has moved in the opposite direction. Because of the liquidity issues in global financial markets, LIBOR rates have actually increased at the same time that treasury and other benchmark yields have been declining, so the Fed lowering rates today would not help too many sub-prime mortgage holders.

Even with lower rates, the home still must appraise for the amount being borrowed plus another 10 to 20%. In most places, depreciation alone has eliminated the opportunity to refinance and take advantage of rate adjustments.

How are Home Equity Lines of Credit Affected?

How about my Home Equity Line of Credit (HELOC): Yes, if you have that home equity line of credit that you used to renovate your bathroom/kitchen recently, then when the Fed lowers rates, your rate comes down as well. That's because HELOCs are predominantly pegged to the prime rate, which moves in step with the Federal Reserve.

Chapter Nine

Life After Short Sale: When You Want To Buy A Home Again..FHA To The Rescue!

Remember, after a short sale, usually it is possible to obtain a new mortgage in as few as 18 to 24 months, assuming all other credit has been kept clean**. Also remember that under strict guidelines, it is possible to do a short-sale and a purchase at the same time.**

Get ready for FHA loans to become the best choice EVEN in the high priced areas like California!

It is now possible to get a FHA Mortgage in certain parts of the country for over $700,000!

You Must Know How FHA Loans Work:

First, it's important to understand that FHA is not only for first time home buyers, anyone can sign up for an FHA loan, as long as you don't have more than one FHA Loan at a time.

Your job is to establish a relationship with an FHA approved lender. Not all lenders hold this qualification.

Little Known SECRETS of FHA Loans:

*FHA Can Help Clients With Blemished Credit

History. New programs are coming out that will allow borrowers with credit score in the high 500s buy a home.

* Bankruptcy. You can obtain an FHA loan two years from the date of your bankruptcy discharge, as long as you've maintained good credit since your debts were discharged.

*Foreclosure. If you keep your credit in excellent shape after a foreclosure, an FHA loan will be available to you two years from the final date of your foreclosure.

Ultra Competitive Rates & Terms

* There is little or no adjustment to the interest rate for an FHA loan, as the rates vary within .125 percent of a conventional loan.

* Mortgage insurance is funded into the loan, meaning a premium of 1.5% is added to the loan balance instead of being paid out-of-pocket. In addition, a small portion for the mortgage insurance premium is added to the monthly payment, but it is far less than private mortgage insurance premiums.

* Qualifying Borrowers can finance 97% of the purchase price and put down 3 percent. In some instances, when combined with other types of loans, the down payment can be zero.

• Allowable debt ratios are higher than the debt-ratio limits imposed for conventional loans.

- Borrowers can get up to 6% back from the seller to help with all of their closing costs.

Forget what you thought you knew about FHA…

At one point, FHA repair demands were so excessive that sellers would discount the list price to buyers who would agree to obtain conventional loans over FHA loans. Today the requirements appear more reasonable.

* You can purchase a home in need of repairs and finance the repair costs with the mortgage. This way you can make the necessary repairs immediately without having to come up with the money yourself.

 * You can purchase manufactured homes and condominiums with a FHA loan.

 * You can finance the cost of energy-efficient repairs with the mortgage.

 * Defective roofs that leak still need to be replaced but an older roof does not necessitate replacement if it doesn't leak. An roofing certification is acceptable in most cases.

  * Windows that stick upon opening or have cracked panes do not require replacement.

 * FHA appraisals do not take the place of a home

inspection, and never have. Buyers should still obtain a professional home inspection.

It's time to take advantage of the return of the FHA loan! It's about to become significantly better than before, with higher limits and an easier appraisal process.

Chapter Ten

Something You Should Know: The Death Of The HELOC....Millions Of Homeowners Shut Out.

Most major lenders are freezing withdrawals from Home Equity Lines of Credit (HELOCs) – and I don't want you to be caught off guard by this development. If you were planning on using your HELOC for spring home improvements or college tuition chances are the money has been shut off.

You should be aware that the lender retains the right to suspend or reduce the line of credit available if your property value falls below the appraised value used to originate the loan. Lenders are actively assessing (performing Broker Price Opinions, or Appraisals) properties and then suspending access for account holders who have seen a downward slide in their home value. Many of our students who do BPOs are reporting to us a dramatic increase in BPO requests from lenders for this reason.

Actual notice from Countrywide...sent to borrowers:

'Important message about your loan: At Countrywide Home Loans we are committed to helping customers sustain homeownership. As part of the commitment, and in keeping with its sound risk-management and responsible lending practices, Countrywide Home Loan is reviewing and analyzing home equity lines of credit in its servicing portfolio.

We believe that the decline in the value of your property, from its original appraised value at the time your loan was made is significant. In accordance with the terms of your Home Equity Credit Line Agreement and Disclosure Statement (Agreement), we have elected to suspend further draws against your account as of the Effective Date above.'

The Los Angeles Times recently reported that Countrywide notified many homeowners they've lost their right to borrow against their credit lines:

'Tens of thousands of homeowners with home equity lines of credit are getting a rude surprise: They've been told by their lender that they can no longer take money out on their credit lines because sinking home prices have left them with little or no equity.

Among the lenders taking such action is Countrywide Financial Corp., which sent 122,000 letters to customers last week telling them they could no longer borrow against their credit lines. In some cases, according to the company, the borrowers are now "upside down" — the total debt on the home exceeds the market value of the property.

Calabasas-based Countrywide, the nation's largest mortgage lender, says it uses computer modeling that factors in changes in home prices to determine which customers will have their money tap shut off.'

If there was any question that consumers were feeling

the pinch before…just wait until they are told that their homes are worth LESS than what they owe. Or in the word of Countrywide, "Significantly Less". Do you think that will have an effect on the economy? Think this will make consumers feel more confident about housing?

Appendix A:

Loss Mitigation Companies and Contact Info.

This is the most complete list of loss mitigation phone numbers for lenders on the Internet. It is sorted in alphabetical order. The first step to stop foreclosure is to contact your lender and try and obtain a reasonable loan workout or repayment plan. The quicker you get the ball rolling, the better chance you have of striking a deal with your lender, so you can save your home and your credit. The hardest call is the first. It only gets easier after that. Time is ticking and it goes by fast when you're behind the infamous 8 ball. As Nike would say, "Just Do It!"

Here's the list:

Lender/Servicer Loss Mitigation Phone Numbers & Contact Information:

ABM AMRO Mortgage (800) 783-8900
Web:
https://www.mortgage.com/C3/application.busAccredit ed Home Lenders (877) 683-4466 AMC Mortgage Services (Also handles loans originated by Ameriquest and Argent) (800) 211-6926
1600 McConnor Parkway
Schaumburg, IL 60173
Web:
https://www.myamcloan.com/malwebapp/begin.do

American Home Mortgage Corp. (877) 304-3100*

Ameriquest Mortgage (Debt collection — see AMC Mortgage Services) (800) 211-6926

Aurora Loan Services (Debt collection) (800) 550-0508
By Overnight Mail:
601 5th Avenue
Scottsbluff, NE 69361
Attn: Customer Service
By Regular Mail:
P.O. Box 1706
Scottsbluff, NE 69363
E-mail: ccnmail@alservices.com
Web: https://www.alservices.com/Consumer/UI/SSL/Authentication/Login.aspx?ReturnUrl=%2fConsumer%2fUI%2fSSL%2fServ icing%2fDefault.aspx

Avelo Mortgage LLC (866) 992-8356*Bank of America (800) 846-2222BB&T Mortgage (800) 827-3722*
AmTrust Bank (aka Ohio Savings Bank) (888) 696-4444

Beneficial (800) 333-5848

Central Pacific Bank (800) 342-8422*

Charter One (800) 234-6002

Chase (800) 548-7912
Loss Mitigation (877) 838-1882 ext 52195 The Number you will be directed to after you give your

loan number: (866) 665-7629 (business hours are 11AM-8PM M-TH, 8AM-12PM F)
Chase Home Finance (800) 848-9136 (customer service) (858) 605-2181 (delinquency customer service)
Chase Home Finance-New Jersey (800) 446-8939*Chevy Chase Bank (800) 933-9100*
Web: https://chaseonline.chase.com/chaseonline/logon/sso_logon.jsp?fromLoc=ALL&LOB=COLLogon

Chase Manhattan Mortgage
(800) 446-8939 (Ohio Servicing Center)
(800) 526-0072 (Florida Servicing Center)
(800) 527-3040 x533 (Florida Servicing Center)Chevy Chase Bank (800) 933-9100
Web: https://www.chevychasebank.com/htm/payment.html (Payment Addresses)Citi Financial Mortgage (800) 753-3673 Citimortgage (800) 283-7918

Countrywide (800) 262-4218
Web: https://customers.countrywide.com/se…t_login254.asp

Ditech (800) 852-0656 (800) 449-8582

Downey Financial Corp. (800) 824-6902, ext. 6696

Deutsche Bank National Call Number on Mortgage Statement

EMC (800) 723-3004
P.O. Box 141358
Irving, TX 75014-1358
Web:
https://www.emcmortgageservicing.com/ccn/ccnsecurity.asp

EverBank (800) 669-7724 ext. 4730

Equity One (Debt collection) (866) 361-3460

First Horizon Home Loans (800) 489-2966*

Fifth Third Bank (800) 375-1745 Option 3

First Merit Bank (888) 728-9931

Flagstar Bank (800) 968-7700, ext. 9780

Fremont Investment & Loan (866) 484-0291

GMAC Mortgage (800) 850-4622

GreenPoint Mortgage Funding (800) 784-5566, ext. 5383*

Green Tree (877) 816-9125

Homecomings Financial (800) 799-9250

HomeEq Mortgage Servicing (Debt collection) (866) 822-1471

Household Finance (An HSBC Co.) (800) 333-5848

Household Mortgage (800) 333-4489

HSBC Mortgage (800) 338-6441
Default Resolution Team (if long term problem)
2929 Walden Avenue
Depew, NY 14043
(888) 648-3124 Loss Mit
(732) 352-7519 Fax
Web:
http://us.hsbc.com/personal/mortgage/existing/difficult
ies.asp

Huntington National Bank (800) 323-4695

Indymac Bank (877) 736-5556
C/O Loan Resolution Department
P.O Box 7014
Pasadena, CA 91107
(Monday - Friday 6:15am-7:15pm. (Pacific Time)
Web:
https://www.indymacbank.com/contactus/loanResoluti
on.asp

Irwin Mortgage (888) 218-1988
P.O Box 7014
Pasadena, CA 91107
Web:
https://www.irwinmortgage.com/wps/portal/!ut/p/cxml/
E-mail:
deliquency.prevention@irwinmortgage.comJames B.
Nutter & Company (800) 315-7334Key Bank (800)

422-2442 LaSalle National Bank (800) 783-8900

Litton Loan Servicing (800) 999-8501 or (800) 548-8665
Fax (713) 966-8820
4828 Loop Central Drive
Houston, Texas 77081-2226
Web: https://www.littonloan.com/index.asp

Loss Mitigation Department Hours:
Monday Eastern: 9 a.m. - 7 p.m. Central:8 a.m. - 6 p.m. Mountain:7 a.m. - 5 p.m. Pacific:6 a.m. - 4 p.m.
Tuesday-Thursday Eastern:9 a.m. - 9 p.m. Central:8 a.m. - 8 p.m. Mountain:7 a.m. - 7 p.m. Pacific:6 a.m. - 6 p.m.
Friday Eastern:10 a.m. - 6 p.m. Central:9 a.m. - 5 p.m. Mountain:8 a.m. - 4 p.m. Pacific:7 a.m. - 3 p.m.
Default Counseling Department representatives are also available most weekends on Saturday from 8 a.m. to 12 p.m. and Sunday from 10 a.m. to 2 p.m. (CST).

Midland Mortgage (800) 552-3000 or (800) 654-4566
Web:
https://www.mymidlandmortgage.com/MyMortgage/Login/Login.asp

Mortgage Lenders Network (800) 691-0129
E-mail: customerservice@mlnusa.com
Web:
http://www.mlnusa.com/customers/info_credithelp.asp
Mortgage Electronic Registration Systems (MERS) (888) 679-6377National City (800) 367-9305, Ext.

53221 or (800) 523-8654
Attention: Homeowner's Assistance
3232 Newmark Dr.
Miamisburg, Ohio 45342
(8AM-10:30PM ET, Monday - Thursday)
(8AM-5PM ET, Friday)
(8AM-Noon, Saturday)
Web:
http://www.nationalcitymortgage.com/service_assista
nce.asp Nationwide Advantage Mortgage Company
(800) 356-3442, ext. 6002*
NationStar Mortgage (888) 850-9398* Press 0 for
operator

New Century Financial Now Carrington Mortgage
Services (800) 790-9502 or (877) 206-9904
(6:00 a.m. to 7:00 p.m. Pacific Time, Monday -
Thursday)
(6:00 a.m. to 6:00 p.m. Pacific Time, Friday)
Web:
https://myloan.newcentury.com/webapps/servicing/my
loans/index.do

NovaStar Mortgage Loan Resolution Department
(888) 743-0774 Non-English: (888) 743-0774, ext.
4523

Ocwen Federal Bank (800) 746-2936 or (877) 596-
8560
Web: http://www.ocwencustomers.com/csc_fa.cfm

Attention: Financial Information
12650 Ingenuity Drive

Orlando, Florida 32826
or
Ocwen Financial Corporation
1661 Worthington Rd., Suite 100
West Palm Beach, Florida 33409
Phone: 877-226-2936

For serving Ocwen with legal process, please send to
their registered agent:
Corporation Service Company
2711 Centerville Road, Suite 400
Wilmington, DE 19808
Phone: 561-682-8000, x8386

Option One (866) 711-1962 or (888) 275-2648
Web:
http://www.oomc.com/servicing/servicing_baifaqs.asp

PHH Mortgage (Formerly Cendant) (800) 257-0460
For borrowers facing possible delinquency: (800) 330-
0423*
For borrowers in the foreclosure process: (800) 750-
2518
Web:https://www.phhmortgage.com/sso/mq/login
ResMae Mortgage Corp. (877) 473-7623, ext. 5944

Saxon (800) 665-7367

Select Portfolio Servicing (888) 818-6032
Fax: (801) 293-3936
Loan Resolution Department
P.O. Box 65250
Salt Lake City, UT 84165-0250

(Monday - Thursday 10:00 a.m. - 10:00 p.m. EST)
(Friday 10:00 a.m. - 7:00 p.m. EST)
(Saturday 9:00 a.m. - 1:00 p.m. EST)
Web:
http://www.spservicing.com/services/customer/loanre
solution.htm

SkyBank (800) 290-3359

Sun Trust Mortgage (800) 634-7928
PO Box 26149
Richmond, VA 23260-6149
Mail Code RVW 3003Web:
https://www.suntrustmortgage.com/generalquestions.
asp#

Third Federal Savings (888) 844-7333

US Bank (800) 365-7900

Wachovia Bank of Delaware (866) 642-8608

Washington Mutual (866) 926-8937 or (888) 453-3102
or (800) 478-0036 or (800) 254-3677

Waterfield Mortgage (800) 957-7245
Fax: (260) 459-5390
c/o Loss Mitigation Dept.
7500 W. Jefferson Blvd.
Fort Wayne, IN 46804
(7 am – 10 pm EST Monday – Thursday)
(7 am – 9 pm EST Fridays)
(8 am – 2 pm EST Saturdays)

E-Mail: saveyourhome@waterfield.com
Web:
http://www.waterfield.com/scripts/cgiip.exe/WService=
wfg/pub/borrowerservices/delqasst

Wells Fargo (877) 216-8448 or (866) 261-5642 or
(800)766-0987 or (800) 678-7986 for payment
assistance
Borrower Counseling Services
Monday - Friday 8:00 a.m. - 9:00 p.m., CT
Saturday 9:00 a.m. - 2:00 p.m., CT
Web: https://www.wellsfargo.com/mortgage/account/

Wendover Financial Services Corporation (800) 934-
1081 or (800) 436-1022
Web: http://www.wendover.com/borrowers.html

Wilshire Credit Corporation (888) 502-0100
P.O. Box 8517
Portland, OR 97207-8517
From 6 a.m. to 5 p.m. (Pacific time) Monday through
Friday
Web: http://www.wfsg.com/borrower/borrower.aspx

*No direct line to the loss mitigation or loan
modification department. But we are working on it

APPENDIX B

What's the difference between Short Sale vs. Short Payoff?

In our current real estate environment it is crucial that to fully understand the difference between a **"Short Sale"** and a **"Short Payoff"**.

A **Short Sale** is where the lender or investor agrees to accept an amount less than actual owed on the property.

The **Criteria for a Short Sale** are that the borrower demonstrates a verifiable long term hardship.

A **Short Payoff** is when the lender agrees to release the lien (their interest) on the property and allow the property to be "conveyed" to a new owner. The lender agrees to accept less than the amount owed on the property to release the lien however they extend a certain amount of "credit" to the borrower in the form of an unsecured line of credit or promissory note. The **Criteria for a Short Payoff** – The mortgage is current, the borrower has great credit, the borrower had and can demonstrate the ability to pay off the debt.

When would you request a Short Payoff? – You would request a short payoff when the home has lost value dramatically and you do not have the ability to pay the large amount to get completely out of the property.

Note – Not all lenders will allow for a Short Payoff, however you will never know if you never ask.

Advantages of a Short Pay-Off:
• You are able to move out of the property and get on with your life.
• You SHOULD receive no negative feedback on your credit.
• You may obtain a lower interest rate on the loan. Sometimes 1-2%.

If for some crazy reason your ability to pay changes and your client are not able to pay on the note, the credit ramifications are significantly smaller.

How to apply for a short payoff
1. If possible call the lender and ask them if they will accept a short payoff. Remember you may need to talk to a supervisor or to loss mitigation directly.
2. Put together your package, this is the same information as your short sale package, *however the goal is to show the lender the abilty to pay not the inability to pay.*
3. Do not accept the first no as the answer, and never paint a lender or servicer with a broad brush. Remember most lenders do not work with just one investor, lenders sell their loans to different investors so if Countrywide says no today that does not mean no tomorrow.

Man in the Arena

"It is not the critic who counts: not the man who points out how the strong man stumbles or where the doer of deeds could have done better. The credit belongs to the man who is actually in the arena, whose face is marred by dust and sweat and blood, who strives valiantly, who errs and comes up short again and again, because there is no effort without error or shortcoming, but who knows the great enthusiasms, the great devotions, who spends himself for a worthy cause; who, at the best, knows, in the end, the triumph of high achievement, and who, at the worst, if he fails, at least he fails while daring greatly, so that his place shall never be with those cold and timid souls who knew neither victory nor defeat." Theodore Roosevelt

APPENDIX C:

The Complete State-by-State Guidebook on the most Common Foreclosure Procedures.

This section is written for the purpose of providing current information in regard to the topics as set forth in the text. It is not the intention of any author or publisher herein, to provide the reader with specific legal, financial, tax, accounting or professional advice. Understand that each business transaction presents a whole different or unique set of circumstances. Each state is different and applicable laws, regulations and terminology for related subjects may vary in different jurisdictions. Considerable efforts are made to provide the reader with timely and accurate information; however there are no guarantees. Therefore, if expert assistance and advice is required, the reader should always seek the services of a competent professional.

The following information was compiled by
www.harrisrealestateuniversity.com
If you have any questions please visit our site.

Alabama*

Alabama is a Non-Judicial State
Power of sale constitutes part of security
Where a power to sell lands is given to the grantee in any mortgage, or other conveyance intended to secure the payment of money, the power is part of the security, and may be executed by any person, or the personal representative of any person who, by assignment or otherwise, becomes entitled to the money thus secured; and a conveyance of the lands sold under such power of sale to the purchaser at the sale, executed by the mortgagee, any assignee or other person entitled to the money thus secured, his agent or attorney, or the auctioneer making the sale, vests the legal title thereto in such purchaser.
Probate judges shall index foreclosure deeds by the names of the original grantor and grantee in the mortgage, and also by the names of the grantor and grantee in the foreclosure deeds.

Sale under power where instrument silent as to place or terms of sale.
If a deed of trust or mortgage, with power of sale, is silent as to the place or terms of sale, or as to the character or mode of notice, a sale may be made at the courthouse door of the county wherein the land is situated, after condition broken, for cash to the highest bidder, after 30 days' notice of the time, place and terms of sale by publishing such notice once a week for four consecutive weeks in a newspaper published in the county wherein said lands or property in said mortgage or deed of trust are situated.

Foreclosure when instrument contains no power of sale. If no power of sale is contained in a mortgage or deed of trust, the grantee or any assignee thereof, at his option, after condition broken, may foreclose same either in a court having jurisdiction of the subject matter, or by selling for cash at the courthouse door of the county where the property is situated, to the highest bidder, the lands embraced in said mortgage or deed of trust, after notice of the time, place, terms and purpose of such sale has been given by four consecutive weekly insertions of such notice in some newspaper published in the county wherein said lands, or a portion thereof are situated.

Additional satisfaction permitted under continuing power of sale.
The sale of any part of the property conveyed by mortgage, either under power of sale contained in the mortgage, or by foreclosure, shall operate as a foreclosure of the mortgage only as to the property sold, and if the mortgage indebtedness is not thereby satisfied in full, the other property contained in the mortgage continues as security for the mortgage debt and there may be a further foreclosure of the mortgage, either by sale under power of sale or by foreclosure.
Every power of sale contained in the mortgages hereafter executed shall, unless otherwise expressly provided therein, be held to give a continuing power of sale authorizing the mortgagee or his assignee after the law day of the mortgage to sell the

mortgaged property from time to time in separate lots or parcels as it comes into his possession.

How notice of sale given.
Notice of said sale shall be given in the manner provided in such mortgage or deed of trust or in this Code in the county where the mortgagor resides and the land, or a part thereof, is located; but, if said mortgagor does not reside in the county where the land or any part thereof is located, then such notice must be published in the county where said land, or any material part thereof, is located; provided, that notice of all sales under powers of sale contained in mortgages and deeds of trust executed after July 1, 1936, where the amount secured is $500.00 or more, shall be given by publication once a week for three successive weeks in some newspaper published in the county in which such land or any portion thereof is Situated, and said notice of sale must give the time, place and terms of said sale, together with a description of the property to be sold.

Notice of sale.
Notice of said sale shall be given in the county where said land is located. Notice of all sales under this article shall be given by publication once a week for three successive weeks in a newspaper published in the county or counties in which such land is located. If there is land under the mortgage in more than one county the publication is to be made in all counties where the land is located.
The notice of sale must give the time, place and terms of said sale, together with a description of the

property. If no newspaper is published in the county where the lands are located, the notice shall be placed in a newspaper published in an adjoining county. The notice shall be published in said adjoining county for three successive weeks.

Place and time for conducting foreclosure by power of sale.
The power to sell lands under this article must be exercised at the appropriate courthouse door considered the front or main door to the courthouse, of the county where the mortgaged land or a substantial and material part thereof, is located. The sale shall be held between the hours of 11 A.M. and 4 P.M. on the day designated for the exercise of the power to sell the land.
*Courtesy of Alabama State Statutes
Alaska*

Alaska is a Non-Judicial State Sale By Trustee.
(a) If a deed of trust is executed conveying real property located in the state to a trustee as security for the payment of an indebtedness and the deed provides that in case of default or noncompliance with the terms of the trust, the trustee may sell the property for condition broken, the trustee, in addition to the right of foreclosure and sale, may execute the trust by sale of the property, upon the conditions and in the manner set forth in the deed of trust, without first securing a decree of foreclosure and order of sale from the court, if the trustee has complied with the notice requirements of this section. If the deed of trust is foreclosed judicially or the note

secured by the deed of trust is sued on and a judgment is obtained by the beneficiary, the beneficiary may not exercise the non-judicial remedies described in this section.

(b) Not less than 30 days after the default and not less than three months before the sale the trustee shall record in the office of the recorder of the recording district in which the trust property is located a notice of default setting out
(1) the name of the trustor, (2) the book and page where
the trust deed is recorded, (3) a description of the trust property, including the property's street address if there is a street address for the property, (4) a statement that a breach of the obligation for which the deed of trust is security has occurred, (5) the nature of the breach, (6) the sum owing on the obligation, (7) the election by the trustee to sell the property to satisfy the obligation,
and (8) the date, time, and place of the sale.
An inaccuracy in the street address may not be used to set aside a sale if the legal description is correct. At any time before the sale, if the default has arisen by failure to make payments required by the trust deed, the default may be cured by payment of the sum in default other than the principal which would not then be due if no default had occurred, plus attorney fees or court costs actually incurred by the trustee due to the default. If under the same trust deed notice of default under this subsection has been recorded two or more times previously and the default has been cured under this subsection, the trustee may

elect to refuse payment and continue the sale.

(c) Within 10 days after recording the notice of default, the trustee shall mail a copy of the notice by certified mail to the last known address of each of the following persons or their legal representatives:
(1) the grantor in the trust deed;
(2) the successor in interest to the grantor whose interest appears of record or of whose interest the trustee or the beneficiary has actual notice, or who is in possession of the property;
(3) any other person in possession of or occupying the property;
(4) any person having a lien or interest subsequent to the interest of the trustee in the trust deed, where the lien or interest appears of record or where the trustee or the beneficiary has actual notice of the lien or interest. The notice may be delivered personally instead of by mail.

(d) If the State of Alaska is a subsequent party, the trustee, in addition to the notice of default, shall give the state a supplemental notice of any state lien existing as of the date of filing the notice of default. This notice must set out, with such particularity as reasonably available information will permit, the nature of the state's lien, including the name and address, if known, of the person whose liability created the lien.
The amount shown on the lien document, the department of the state government involved, the recording district, and the book and page on which the lien was recorded.

Sale at Public Auction.

 (a) The sale shall be made under the terms and conditions and in the manner set out in the deed of trust. However, the sale shall be made

(1) at public auction held at the front door of a courthouse of the superior court in the judicial district where the property is located, unless the deed of trust specifically provides that the sale shall be held in a different place; and

(2) after public notice of the time and place of the sale has been given in the manner provided by law for the sale of real property on execution.

(b) The attorney for the trustee may conduct the sale and act in the sale as the auctioneer for the trustee. Sale shall be made to the highest and best bidder. The beneficiary under the trust deed may bid at the trustee's sale. The trustee shall execute and deliver to the purchaser a deed to the property sold.

(c) The deed must recite the date and the book and page of the recording of default, and the mailing or delivery of the copies of the notice of default, the true consideration for the conveyance, the time and place of the publication of notice of sale, and the time, place, and manner of sale, and refer to the deed of trust by reference to the page, volume, and place of record.

(d) After the sale an affidavit of mailing the notice of default and an affidavit of publication of the notice of sale shall be recorded in the mortgage records of the recording district where the property is located.

(e) The trustee may postpone sale of all or any portion of the property by delivering to the person conducting the sale a written and signed request for the postponement to a stated date and hour.

The person conducting the sale shall publicly announce the postponement to the stated date and hour at the time and place originally fixed for the sale. This procedure shall be followed in any succeeding postponement.

Title, Interest, Possessory Rights, and Redemption.
(a) The sale and conveyance transfers all title and interest that the party executing the deed of
trust had in the property sold at the time of its execution, together with all title and interest that party may have acquired before the sale, and the party executing the deed of trust or the heirs or assigns of that party have no right or privilege to redeem the property, unless the deed of
trust so declares.

(b) The purchaser at a sale and the heirs and assigns of the purchaser are, after the execution of a deed to the purchaser by the trustee, entitled to the possession of the premises described in the deed as against the party executing the deed of trust or any other person claiming by, through or under that party, after recording the deed of trust in the recording district where the property is located.

(c) A recital of compliance with all requirements of law regarding the mailing or personal delivery of copies of notices of default in the deed executed under a power of sale is prima facie evidence of compliance with the requirements. The recital is conclusive evidence of compliance with the requirements in favor of a bona fide purchaser or encumbrancer for value and without notice.

Deficiency Judgment Prohibited.
When a sale is made by a trustee under a deed of trust, no other or further action or proceeding may be taken nor judgment entered against the maker or the surety or guarantor of the maker, on the obligation secured by the deed of trust for a deficiency.
*Courtesy of Alaska State Statutes

Arizona*

Arizona is a Power of Sale State
Foreclosure of mortgage by court action
Mortgages of real property and deeds of trust shall be foreclosed by action in a court.

Right of junior lien holder upon foreclosure action by senior lien holder
Any time after an action to foreclose a mortgage or

deed of trust is brought, and prior to the sale, a person having a junior lien on the property shall be entitled to an assignment of all the interest of the holder of the mortgage or deed of trust by paying him the amount secured, with interest and costs, together with the amount of any other superior liens of the same holder. The assignee may then continue the action in his name.

Judgment of foreclosure; contents; sale of property; resale

A. When a mortgage or deed of trust is foreclosed, the court shall give judgment for the entire amount determined due, and shall direct the mortgaged property, or as much thereof as is necessary to satisfy the judgment, to be sold.

B. Judgments for the foreclosure of mortgages and other liens shall provide that the plaintiff recover his debt, damages and costs, with a foreclosure of the plaintiff's lien on the property subject to the lien, and, except in judgments against executors, administrators and guardians, that a special execution issue to the sheriff or any constable of the county where the property is located, directing him to seize and sell the property as under execution, in satisfaction of the judgment.

If the property cannot be found, or if the proceeds of the sale are insufficient to satisfy the judgment, then if so ordered by the court the sheriff shall take the money or any balance thereof remaining unpaid out of any other property of the defendant. Any sale of real property to satisfy a judgment shall be a credit on the judgment in the amount of either the fair market value of the real property or the sale price of the real property at sheriff's sale, whichever is greater.

C. If the debt for which the lien is held is not all due, as soon as enough of the property is sold to pay the amount due, with costs, the sale shall cease, and afterward as often as more becomes due for principal and interest, the court may, on motion, order more property sold. If the property cannot be sold in portions without injury to the parties, the whole may be ordered sold in the first instance and the entire debt and costs paid, allowing a rebate of interest where proper.

Notice of trustee's sale
A. The trustee shall give written notice of the time and place of sale legally describing the trust property to be sold by each of the following methods:
　　1. Recording a notice in the office of the recorder of each county where the trust property is situated.
　　2. Giving notice as provided in section 33-809 to the extent applicable.
　　3. Posting a notice, at least twenty days before the date of sale in some conspicuous place on the trust property to be sold, if posting can be accomplished without a breach of the peace. If access to the trust property is denied because a common entrance to the property is restricted by a limited access gate or similar impediment, the property shall be posted by posting notice at that gate or impediment.
Notice shall also be posted at one of the places provided for posting public notices at any building that

serves as a location of the superior court in the county where the trust property is to be sold. Posting is deemed completed on the date the first notice is posted.

A. Publication of sale notice in a newspaper of general circulation in each county in which trust property to be sold is situated. Sale notice shall be published at least once a week for four consecutive weeks. The last date of publication shall not be less than ten days prior to the date of sale. Publication is deemed completed on the date of the first publication of notice pursuant to this paragraph.

B. The sale shall be held at the time and place designated in the notice of sale on a day other than a Saturday or legal holiday between 9:00 a.m. and 5:00 p.m. at a specified place on the trust property, at a specified place at any building that serves as a location of the superior court or at a specified place at a place of business of the trustee, in any county in which part of the trust property to be sold is situated.

C. The notice of sale shall contain:
1. The date, time and place of the sale. This date shall be at least ninety days after the date that the notice of sale was recorded.

2. The street address, if any, or identifiable location as well as the legal description of the trust property.

3. The county assessor's tax parcel number for the

trust property or the tax parcel number of a larger parcel of which the trust property is a part.

4. The original principal balance as shown on the deed of trust. If the amount is not shown on the deed of trust, it shall be listed as "unspecified".

5. The names and addresses, as of the date the notice of sale is recorded, of the beneficiary and the trustee, the name and address of the original trustor as stated in the deed of trust, the signature of the trustee and the basis for the trustee's qualification pursuant to section 33-803, subsection   A. The address of the beneficiary shall not be in care of the trustee or trustee's agent.

 6. The telephone number of the trustee.

Sale by public auction; postponement of sale
A. On the date and at the time and place designated in the notice of sale, the trustee shall offer to sell the trust property at public auction for cash to the highest bidder. The attorney or agent for the trustee may conduct the sale and act at such sale as the auctioneer for the trustee. Any person, including the trustee or beneficiary, may bid at the sale.
Only the beneficiary may make a credit bid in lieu of cash at sale. The trustee shall require every bidder except the beneficiary to provide a one thousand dollar deposit in cash or in any other form that is satisfactory to the trustee as a condition of entering a bid.
The trustee shall not refuse cash as a form of

payment of the bidder's deposit. Every bid shall be deemed an irrevocable offer until the sale is completed, except that a subsequent bid by the same bidder for a higher amount shall cancel that bidder's lower bid.

To determine the highest price bid, the trustor or beneficiary present at the sale may recommend the manner in which the known lots, parcels or divisions of the trust property be sold. The trustee shall conditionally sell the trust property under each recommendation, and, in addition, shall conditionally sell the trust property as a whole.

The trustee shall determine which conditional sale or sales result in the highest total price bid for all of the trust property. The trustee shall return deposits to all but the bidder or bidders whose bid or bids result in the highest bid price.

The sale shall be completed on payment by the purchaser of the price bid in a form satisfactory to the trustee.

The subsequent execution, delivery and recordation of the trustee's deed as prescribed by section 33811 are ministerial acts. If the trustee's deed is recorded in the county in which the trust property is located within fifteen business days after the date of the sale, the trustee's sale is deemed perfected at the appointed date and time of the trustee's sale.

B. The person conducting the sale may, for any cause deemed in the interest of the beneficiary or trustor, or both, postpone or continue the sale from time to time or change the place of the sale to any other location authorized pursuant to this chapter by giving notice of the new date, time and place by public declaration at the time and place last appointed for the sale. Any new sale date shall be a fixed date within ninety calendar days of the date of the declaration. No other notice of the postponed, continued or relocated sale is required except as provided in subsection C of this section.

C. A sale shall not be complete if the sale as held is contrary to or in violation of any federal statute in effect because of an unknown or undisclosed bankruptcy.

A sale so held shall be deemed to be continued to a date, time and place announced by the trustee at the sale and shall comply with subsection B of this section or, if not announced, shall be continued to the same place and at the same time twenty-eight days later, unless the twenty-eighth day falls on a Saturday or legal holiday, in which event it shall be continued to the first business day thereafter.

In the event a sale is continued because of an unknown or undisclosed bankruptcy, the trustee shall notify by registered or certified mail, with postage prepaid, all bidders who provide their names, addresses and telephone numbers in writing to the party conducting the sale of the continuation of the sale.

Redemption of property by payment to officer directed under foreclosure judgment to sell the property.

If payment is made to the officer directed to sell mortgaged property under a foreclosure judgment, before the foreclosure sale takes place, the officer shall make a certificate of payment and acknowledge it, and the certificate shall be recorded in the office in which the mortgage or deed of trust is recorded.

Payment of bid; trustee's deed

A. The highest bidder at the sale, other than the beneficiary to the extent of the credit bid, shall pay the price bid by no later than 5:00 p.m. of the following day, other than a Saturday or legal holiday. If the highest bidder fails to pay the amount bid for the property struck off to the bidder at the sale, the trustee, in the trustee's sole discretion, shall either continue the sale to reopen bidding or immediately offer the trust property to the second highest bidder who may purchase the trust property at that bidder's bid price.

The deposit of the highest bidder who fails to pay the amount bid shall be forfeited and shall be treated as additional sale proceeds to be applied. If the second highest bidder does not pay that bidder's bid price by 5:00 of the next day excluding Saturdays and legal holidays after the property has been offered to that bidder by the trustee, the trustee shall either continue the sale to reopen bidding or offer the trust property to each of the prior bidders on successive days excluding Saturdays and legal holidays in order of their highest bid, until a bid price is paid, or if there is no other bidder, the sale shall be deemed to be continued to a time and place designated by the trustee, or if not designated, the sale shall be continued to the same place and at the same time twenty-eight days after the last scheduled sale date.

If the twenty-eighth day is a Saturday or legal holiday, the sale shall be continued to the next business day. If the sale is continued, the trustee shall provide notice of the continuation of the sale by registered or certified mail, with postage prepaid, to all bidders who provide their names, addresses and telephone numbers in writing to the party conducting the sale. In addition to the forfeit of deposit, a highest bidder who fails to pay the amount bid by that bidder is liable to any person who suffers loss or expenses as a result, including attorney fees.

In any subsequent sale of trust property, the trustee may reject any bid of that person. In any sale that is continued pursuant to this subsection, the trustee shall reject the bid from any previous bidder who elected not to pay that bidder's bid price.

The price bid shall be paid at the office of the trustee or the trustee's agent, or any other reasonable place designated by the trustee. The payment of the bid price may be made at a later time if agreed upon in writing by the trustee.

The trustee shall execute and deliver the trustee's deed to the purchaser within seven business days after receipt of payment by the trustee or the trustee's agent made in a form that is satisfactory to the trustee.

The trustee's deed shall raise the presumption of compliance with the requirements of the deed of trust and this chapter relating to the exercise of the power of sale and the sale of the trust property, including recording, mailing, publishing and posting of notice of sale and the conduct of the sale.

A trustee's deed shall constitute conclusive evidence of the
meeting of those requirements in favor of purchasers or encumbrances for value and without actual notice. Knowledge of the trustee shall not be imputed to the beneficiary.

C. The trustor, its successors or assigns, and all persons to whom the trustee mails a notice of a sale under a trust deed pursuant to section 33-809 shall waive all defenses and objections to the sale not raised in an action that results in the issuance of a court order granting relief pursuant to rule 65, **Arizona rules of civil procedure**, entered before 5:00 p.m. on the last day other than Saturday, Sunday or other legal holiday before the scheduled date of the sale.

A copy of the order, the application for the order and the complaint shall be delivered to the trustee within twenty-four hours after entering the
order.

D. A sale is not complete if the sale violates subsection C of this section because of an undisclosed order entered by the court within the time provided for in subsection C of this section.

A sale held in violation of subsection C of this section shall be continued to a date, time and place announced by the trustee at the sale and shall comply with section 33-810, subsection B.

If not announced, the sale shall be continued to the same place and at the same time twenty-eight days later. If the twenty-eighth day falls on a Saturday, Sunday or other legal holiday, the sale shall be continued to the next business day. If the sale is continued because of an unknown or undisclosed order as provided in this subsection, the trustee shall notify by registered or certified mail, with postage prepaid, all bidders who provide names, addresses and telephone numbers in writing to the party conducting the sale of the continuation of the sale.

E. The trustee's deed shall operate to convey to the purchaser the title, interest and claim of the trustee, the trustor, the beneficiary, their respective successors in interest and all persons claiming the trust property sold by or through them, including all interest or claim in the trust property acquired subsequent to the recording of the deed of trust and prior to delivery of the trustee's deed. That conveyance shall be absolute without right of redemption and clear of all liens, claims or interests that have a priority subordinate to the deed of trust and shall be subject to all liens, claims or interests that have a priority senior to the deed of trust.

Disposition of proceeds of sale

A. The trustee shall apply the proceeds of the trustee's sale in the following order of priority:

 1. To the costs and expenses of exercising the power of sale and the sale, including the payment of the trustee's fees and reasonable attorney's fees actually incurred.

2. To the payment of the contract or contracts secured by the trust deed.

3. To the payment of all other obligations provided in or secured by the trust deed and

actually paid by the beneficiary before the trustee's sale.

4. To the junior lien holders or encumbrancers in order of their priority as they existed at the time of the sale. After payment in full to all junior lien holders and encumbrancers payment shall be made to the trustor, except that if the trustor has sold or transferred the property to another owner before the trustee's sale, payment shall be made to the person who is the owner of record at the time of the trustee's sale.

*Courtesy of Arizona State Statutes

Arkansas*

Arkansas is a Judicial and Non-Judicial State. Judicial is most commonly used. Qualifications of trustee-Appointment of successor trustee.

A. A trustee of a deed of trust shall be any:

1. Attorney who is an active licensed member of the Bar of the Supreme Court of the State of Arkansas or law firm among whose members includes such an attorney;

2. Bank or savings and loan association authorized to do business under the laws of Arkansas or those of the United States;

3. Corporation which is an affiliate of a bank or savings and loan association authorized to do business under the laws of Arkansas or those of the United States, which is either an Arkansas bank or a registered out-of-state bank which maintains a branch in the State of Arkansas; or

4. Agency or authority of the State of Arkansas where not otherwise prohibited by law.

The beneficiary may appoint a successor trustee at any time by filing a substitution of trustee for record with the recorder of the county in which the trust property is situated.

The new trustee shall succeed to all the power, duties, authority, and title of the original trustee and any previous
successor trustee. The beneficiary may, by express provision in the substitution of a trustee, ratify and confirm actions taken on its behalf by the new trustee prior to the recording of the substitution of the trustee.

The substitution shall identify the deed of trust by stating the names of the original parties thereto, the date of recordation, and the book and page where recorded or the recorder's document number. The substitution shall also state the name of the new trustee and shall be executed and duly acknowledged by all the beneficiaries or their successors in interest.

A mortgagee may delegate his or her powers and duties under this chapter to an attorney-in-fact, whose acts shall be done in the name of and on behalf of the mortgagee. The qualifications for an attorney-in-fact shall be the same as those for a trustee.

The appointment of an attorney-in- fact by a mortgagee shall be made by a duly executed, acknowledged, and recorded power of attorney, which shall identify the mortgage by stating the names of the original parties thereto, the date of recordation, and the book and page where recorded or the recorder's document number.

A substitution of trustee or power of attorney shall be recorded before any trustee's or mortgagee's deed executed by the substituted trustee or attorney-in-fact is recorded.

Conditions to exercise of power.
A trustee or mortgagee may not sell the trust property unless:
1. The deed of trust or mortgage is filed for record with the recorder of the county in which the trust property is situated;

2. There is a default by the mortgagor, grantor, or other person owing an obligation, the performance of which obligation is secured by the mortgage or deed of trust or by their successors in interest with respect to any provision in the mortgage or deed of trust that authorizes sale in the event of default of the provision.

3. The mortgagee, trustee, or beneficiary has filed for record with the recorder of the county in which the trust property is situated a duly acknowledged notice of default and intention to sell.

4. No action has been instituted to recover the debt or any part of it secured by the mortgage or deed of trust or, if such action has been instituted, the action has been dismissed; and
5. A period of at least sixty (60) days has elapsed since the recording of the notice of default and intention to sell.

Contents of notice -Persons to receive notice.

A. The mortgagee's or trustee's notice of default and intention to sell shall set forth:

1. The names of the parties to the mortgage or deed of trust;

2. A legal description of the trust property and, if applicable, the street address of the property;

3. The book and page numbers where the mortgage or deed of trust is recorded or the recorder's document number;

4. The default for which foreclosure is made;

5. The mortgagee's or trustee's intention to sell the trust property to satisfy the obligation, including in conspicuous type a warning as follows: "YOU MAY LOSE YOUR PROPERTY, IF YOU DO NOT TAKE IMMEDIATE ACTION"; and

6. The time, date, and place of sale.

The mortgagee's or trustee's notice of default and intention to sell shall be mailed within thirty (30) days of the recording of the notice by certified mail, postage prepaid and by first class mail, postage prepaid, to the address last known to the mortgagee or the trustee or beneficiary of the following persons:

1. The mortgagor or grantor of the deed of trust;

2. Any successor in interest to the mortgagor or grantor whose interest appears of record or whose interest the mortgagee or the trustee or beneficiary has actual notice;

3. Any person having a lien or interest subsequent to the interest of the mortgagee or trustee when that lien

or interest appears of record or when the mortgagee, the trustee, or the beneficiary has actual notice of the lien or interest; and

4. Any person requesting notice.
The disability, incapacity, or death of any person to whom notice must be given under this section shall not delay or impair in any way the mortgagee's or trustee's right to proceed with a sale, provided that the notice has been given in the manner required by this section to the guardian or conservator or to the administrator or executor, as the case may be.

Publication of notice.
The mortgagee or trustee shall publish the notice:
1. In a newspaper of general circulation in the county in which the trust property is situated or in a newspaper of general statewide daily publication one (1) time a week for four (4) consecutive weeks prior to the date of sale.

The final publication shall be no more than ten (10) days prior to the sale; By employing a third-party posting provider to post notice at the place at the county courthouse where foreclosure sales are customarily advertised and conducted; and By employing a third- party Internet foreclosure sale notice information service provider.

On or before the date the mortgagee or trustee conducts the sale, a duly acknowledged affidavit of mailing and publication of the notice of default and intention to sell shall be filed for record with the recorder of the county in which the trust property is situated.

Manner of sale.
The sale shall be held on the date and at the time and place designated in the notice of default and intention to sell, except that the sale shall:
1. Be held between 9:00 a.m. and 4:00 p.m.;
2. Be held either at the premises of the trust property or at the front door of the county courthouse of the county in which the trust property is situated; and
3. Not be held on a Saturday, Sunday, or a legal holiday.
Any person, including the mortgagee and the beneficiary, may bid at the sale. The trustee may bid for the beneficiary but not for himself or herself.
The mortgagee or trustee shall engage a third party to conduct the sale and act at the sale as the auctioneer of the mortgagee or trustee. No bid shall be accepted that is less than two-thirds (2/3) of the entire indebtedness due at the date of sale.
The person conducting the sale may postpone the sale from time to time. In every such case, notice of postponement shall be given by:

1. Public proclamation thereof by that person; or

2. Written notice of postponement posted at the time and place last appointed for the sale. No other notice of the postponement need be given unless the sale is postponed for longer than thirty (30) days beyond the

date designated in the notice.

Unless otherwise agreed to by the trustee or mortgagee, the purchaser shall pay at the time of sale the price bid. Interest shall accrue on any unpaid balance of the price bid at the rate specified in the note secured by the mortgage or deed of trust.

Within ten (10) days after the sale, the mortgagee or trustee shall execute and deliver the trustee's deed or mortgagee's deed to the purchaser.

The mortgagee or beneficiary shall receive a credit on its bid for:

1. The amount representing the unpaid principal owed;
2. Accrued interest as of the date of the sale;
3. Advances for the payment of taxes, insurance, and maintenance of the trust property; and
4. Costs of the sale, including reasonable trustee's and attorney's fees. The purchaser at the sale shall be entitled to immediate possession of the property.

Possession may be obtained by filing a complaint in the circuit court of the county in which the property lies and attaching a copy of the recorded trustee's or mortgagee's deed, whereupon the purchaser shall be entitled to an ex parte writ of assistance. Alternatively, the purchaser may bring an action for forcible entry and detainer.

Effect of sale.

A sale made by a mortgagee or trustee shall foreclose and terminate all interest in the trust property of all persons to whom notice is given and of any other person claiming by, through, or under the person. A failure to give notice to any person entitled to notice shall not affect the validity of the sale as to persons notified.

A person entitled to notice, but not given notice, shall have the rights of a person not made a defendant in a judicial foreclosure.

A sale shall terminate all rights of redemption, and no person shall have a right to redeem the trust property after a sale, notwithstanding that the deed to and possession of the trust property have yet to be delivered.

No notice shall be required to be given to any person claiming an interest subsequent to the filing of the notice of default and intention to sell. The filing of the notice of default and intention to sell shall have the same force and effect as the filing of a lis pendens in a judicial proceeding.

Disposition of proceeds of sale.

The trustee or mortgagee shall apply the proceeds of the sale as follows:

1. To the expenses of the sale, including compensation of the trustee or mortgagee and a reasonable fee by the attorney;

2. To the indebtedness owed;

3. To all persons having recorded liens subsequent to the interest of the trustee or mortgagee as their interests may appear in the order of the priority; and

4. The surplus, if any, to the grantor of the trust deed or to the successor in interest of the grantor entitled to the surplus.

Deficiency judgment.

At any time within twelve (12) months after a sale under this chapter, a money judgment may be sought for the balance due upon the obligation for which a mortgage or deed of trust was given as security.In such action, the plaintiff shall set forth in his or her complaint, and shall have the burden of proving, the entire amount of indebtedness which was secured by the mortgage or deed of trust, the amount for which the trust property was sold, and the fair market value of the trust property at the date of sale, together with interest from the date of sale, costs, and attorney's fees.

A. Judgment shall not exceed the lesser of the following:
1. The amount for which the indebtedness due at the date of sale, with interest from the date of sale, costs, and trustee's and attorney's fees, exceeds the fair market value of the trust property; or
2. The amount for which the indebtedness due at the date of sale, with interest from the date of sale, costs, and trustee's and attorney's fees, exceeds the amount for which the trust property was sold.
*Courtesy of Arkansas State Statutes

California*

California is a Non-Judicial State.

**Day 1,   Day 90,   Day 120, Day 141,
Redemption Period, Publication Period,
Trustee's Sale**
Lasts 90 days from the recordation of the Notice of Default
Lasts 30 days from the end of Held 21 days after first Redemption publication

Redemption Period
Once the Notice of Default records the foreclosure time frame begins. Within 10 business days a copy of the recorded Notice of Default is sent by certified and regular mail to the borrowers at all addresses provided and any recorded special requests. Within 30 days a copy of the Notice of Default is sent by certified and regular mail to new owners and all junior lien holders to the Deed of Trust being foreclosed.
A Trustee's Sale Guarantee Report is ordered from the title company providing all title information. The foreclosure remains dormant for the next 60 days unless the borrower makes contact to cure.

Publication Period
The publication period begins once the redemption period has expired. A Notice of Trustee's Sale is prepared and published in an adjudicated paper of general circulation in the city in which the property is located.
The Notice of Trustee's Sale is published one time per

week for three weeks. The actual Sale is established by adding at least 20 days to the date that the Notice of Trustee's Sale was first published in the newspaper.

The Notice of Trustee's Sale is posted on the property and in a public place. At least 14 days period to Sale date the Notice of Trustee's Sale must be recorded in the county in which the property is located.

Trustee's Sale
On the day that was established for sale of the property, and only after all publication period requirements have been met, the property is sold to the highest bidder for cash for the full amount of the debt plus foreclosure fee and expenses. If no one bids at the Trustee's Sale, the property automatically reverts back to the beneficiary for the debt.

A Trustee's Deed Upon Sale is recorded in the county in which the property is located transferring title to the foreclosing beneficiary allowing the marketing of the property to recover their debt.

All sales under a power of sale in a deed of trust will be made between the hours of 9:00 a.m. and 5:00 p.m. on any business day, Monday through Friday, at the time specified in the notice of trustee sale.

The sale must be made a public auction to the highest bidder. The trustee has the right to require every bidder to show evidence of ability to pay the full bid in cash, cashier's check or certain bank checks. Each bid is by law an irrevocable offer to purchase.

However, a higher bid cancels an earlier bid. It is unlawful and a criminal offense (a fine of $10,000 or up to one year in jail) to offer anyone consideration not to bid, or to fix or restrain the bidding process in any manner.

 Debtors may reinstate up to five days before non-judicial foreclosure sale. Junior lien holders may no longer redeem, so they may try to protect themselves by:
(1) Advancing funds to bring the senior loan payments current, then foreclosing for the sums advanced;
(2) Bidding at the foreclosure sale so the price will be sufficient to payoff the senior and the junior liens; or
(3) Acquire the property by bidding at the foreclosure. If the debtor has a right to redeem and does so, the junior who purchased the home must be reimbursed. Junior liens do not reattach the property if a borrower redeems a senior lien whose foreclosure extinguished the junior.

This helps borrowers by encouraging the junior to bid up to the property to fair market value at the foreclosure sale, or else lose out, giving borrowers closer to fair value at sale. Lenders may not seek a deficiency judgment if
(1) the foreclosure is non-judicial or if
(2) foreclosure is on a purchase money obligation. The same rules do not apply to guarantee or later lien holders. The lenders may seize alternative collateral.
If the lender forecloses by filing a lawsuit, then the lender can obtain both a foreclosure sale order and a judgment against the borrower for a deficiency after the court ordered sale, but only for the difference between the judgment and the fair value of the

security.

VA Loans

An appraisal should be ordered through an authorized VA appraiser 60 days from the recording of the Notice of Default. A completed VA567 from should be sent to the local VA office with a copy of the Notice of Trustee's Sale and Trustee's Sale Guarantee once publication of the Notice
of Trustee's Sale has begun.

A Corporation Grant Deed should be prepared conveying title from the foreclosing beneficiary to the proper governmental agency.

FHA Loans

A Notice to Occupant of Pending Acquisition should be mailed to mortgagee with a copy of the cover letter to the local FHA office.

A Corporation Grant Deed should be prepared conveying title from the foreclosing beneficiary to the proper governmental agency. If the property is occupied, an eviction process must be started to convey the title to FHA unoccupied.

Once eviction complete, record Corporation Grant Deed and issue title package to FHA for Title Approval Record Corporation Grant Deed and issue FHA 27011 Part A.

*Courtesy of National Foreclosure Professionals and California State Statutes

Colorado*

Colorado is a Non-Judicial State

Notice of Sale
The public trustee, within twenty days after the date of the first publication of the notice of sale, shall mail a copy of such notice as it appeared in a newspaper of general circulation to the grantor at the address given in the deed of trust.

And the public trustee shall also mail a like notice to each person who appears to have acquired a record interest in the property described in such notice of sale subsequent to the recording of such deed of trust, whether by deed, mortgage, judgment, or any other instrument of record.

And, if the foreclosing party has a lien with priority over the lessee or lessees who have unrecorded possessory interests in the property being foreclosed and desires to terminate such possessory interests with the foreclosure, as

evidenced by the inclusion of the names of the lessee or lessees or the occupant or occupants in the list supplied the public trustee pursuant to subsection

(1) of this section, the public trustee shall also mail such a notice to the lessee or lessees of the premises as provided in section 38- 38-305 (1.5).

Such notice shall be mailed to such person at the address given in the recorded instrument, or, if such notice is being sent to the lessee or lessees of the premises, such notice shall be mailed as provided in section 38-38-305 (1.5).

Postage costs under this section shall be part of foreclosure costs. If such recorded instrument does not give such address or if only the county and state are given as the address of such person, it will not be necessary to mail any notice to such person.

It is not necessary to mail a copy of said printed notice to any person whose interest does not appear of record at the time said notice of election and demand for sale is recorded.

Announcement at public trustee's sale.

At any foreclosure sale by a public trustee, the public trustee shall be required to read only the public trustee's number of the proceeding for the sale, the name of the grantor, the street address, if known, and legal description of the property, the name of the owner of the evidence of debt. The date of the sale, the date on which the notice was issued, and the first and last publication dates of the notice. In lieu of reading the legal description, the public trustee may display the legal description to those present at the sale.

Combined notice of right to cure and right to redeem

Within twenty days after the recording of the notice of election and demand for sale by the public, or not less than sixteen nor more than twenty-five days after the entry of a decree of foreclosure or the issuance of a writ of execution directing the sheriff to sell real property.

The public trustee or sheriff shall mail a notice to the grantors of the deed of trust or mortgage being foreclosed, to any subsequent owners of the property being foreclosed, to the current owner of the property being sold, and to any other person having a right to cure a default or a right to redeem the property subject to foreclosure such notice shall contain:

1. The names of the grantors of the deed of trust or mortgage and the original beneficiaries or grantees thereof;

2. The name of the current owner of an evidence of debt secured by the deed of trust or mortgage being foreclosed or the owner of the lien being foreclosed;

3. A statement that the notice of intention to redeem shall be filed at least fifteen calendar days prior to the end of the owner's redemption period;

4. A statement that the notice of intent to cure shall be filed at least fifteen calendar days prior to the date upon which the foreclosure sale is set; and

5. The names, addresses, and telephone numbers of the attorneys, if any, representing the foreclosing lienor.

The combined notice required shall be mailed to those persons who have a right to cure or redeem pursuant to an instrument evidencing such right which was recorded with the county clerk and recorder of the county in which said property is located subsequent to the recording of the deed of trust, mortgage, or other lien being foreclosed and prior to the recording of the notice of election and demand for sale or notice of commencement of the pending foreclosure action (lis pendens).

Such combined notice shall be mailed to such persons at their respective addresses shown in the recorded instruments through which their rights to cure or redeem are derived. Postage costs under this section shall be part of the foreclosure costs.

Court order authorizing sale mandatory.
In all cases of foreclosure of property by the public trustee pursuant to a power of sale contained in a deed of trust, the owner of an evidence of debt secured thereby shall obtain an order authorizing sale from a court properly having jurisdiction to issue the same.
Such order shall be dated, or recite that the hearing was completed, on or before the day prior to the last day on which an effective notice of intention to cure may be filed with the public trustee.

In no event shall the public trustee sell the subject property prior to the issuance of such an order authorizing the sale.

Written bid required -form of bid.
The owner of an evidence of debt secured by a deed of trust, mortgage, or other lien being foreclosed in accordance with the provisions of this article and article 37 of this title, or the attorney or agent for such owner or holder, shall submit, before 12 noon on or before the day prior to the date of sale, a written bid to the public trustee or sheriff as provided in this section.
The owner of such evidence of debt shall bid at least such owner's good faith estimate of the fair market value of the property being sold (less the amount of

unpaid real property taxes and all amounts secured by liens against the property being sold which are senior to the lien being foreclosed and less the estimated reasonable costs and expenses, net of income, of holding, marketing, and selling such property); except that such owner need not bid more than the amount due under such evidence of debt as itemized on the written bid pursuant to subsection (2) of this section.

The failure of the owner of such evidence of debt to bid at least such owner's good faith estimate of the fair market value of the property being sold shall not affect the validity of such foreclosure sale but may be raised as a defense by any person sued on a deficiency.
Such owner or his attorney or agent need not personally attend the foreclosure sale. If such written bid is not timely submitted, the public trustee or sheriff shall continue the sale no longer than two weeks and shall announce the continuance at the time and place designated for the sale.

1. Any written bid submitted to the public trustee or sheriff shall be signed by such owner or by the attorney for such owner and shall set forth an itemization of all amounts due under the evidence of debt and deed of trust, mortgage or other lien being foreclosed, and all costs and expenses allowable by the evidence of debt, deed of trust, mortgage, or other lien being foreclosed, reasonable attorney fees, and

costs incurred by such owner or the attorney for such owner in enforcing the owner's lien or in defending, protecting, and insuring the owners interest in the foreclosed property or any improvements located thereon.

Bids shall be in substantially the following form:
BID
To:

_____

_____

_____

_____

(Public Trustee)*(Sheriff)* of the County of, State of Colorado.

Date: _____
_____, whose mailing address is, bids the sum of $_____in your Sale No. ___
to be held on the day of, 20____ .

The following is an itemization of all amounts due the owner of the evidence of debt secured by the (deed of trust) (mortgage) (lien) being foreclosed. (Inapplicable items may be omitted):

Principal Interest	$_____
Late charges	$_____
Less Impound account credit	$_____
Plus impound account deficiency	$_____
Title or abstracting charges	$_____

Docket fee Appraisal fee $_____
Statutory notice costs $_____
Postage $_____
Photocopies $_____
Attorney fees $_____
Telephone charges $_____
Insurance premiums $_____
Other (describe):
Total due holder $_____
(Public Trustee's)*(Sheriff's)* fees and costs$_____
Publication costs
$_____
Total $_____
Bid $_____
Deficiency $_____

I enclose herewith the following:
1. Order authorizing sale. $_____
2. Check to your order in the sum of $_____
covering the balance of your fees.
 3. Other: $_____

 Please send us the following:
1. Original Certificate of Purchase.'* $_____
2. Promissory Note (with deficiency noted thereon). '*
$_____
3. Refund Check for overpayment of (Public
Trustee's) *(Sheriff's)* costs if any. $_____
4. Other: $_____
'*Delete as case may be.
Name of foreclosing party, agent, or attorney
       By: _____
       Address: _____

Telephone: _____

The public trustee or sheriff shall enter such bid by reading the bid amount set forth on the written bid and the name of the person or entity who submitted such bid.
Bids submitted pursuant to this section may be withdrawn or amended by any person authorized to submit a bid in writing, prior to the date specified in said subsection or orally, at the time of sale.
If a bid is modified orally at the time of sale, the person making such bid shall immediately note such modification on the written itemization thereof and re-execute same.

Fees charged against grantor.
All fees, charges, and costs of every kind and nature incurred under the provisions of articles 37 to 39 of this title shall be an expense of the foreclosure sale chargeable as additional amounts owing under the deed of trust, mortgage, or other lien being foreclosed.
Such amounts shall be deducted from the proceeds of any foreclosure sale, or, if there are not cash proceeds at such sale adequate to pay such amounts, to the extent of such inadequacy, such amounts shall be paid by the owner of the evidence of debt secured by the deed of trust, mortgage, or other lien being foreclosed.

The public trustee or sheriff may require that the owner of the evidence of debt secured by the deed of trust, mortgage, or other lien to be foreclosed deposit with the public trustee or sheriff at the time the notice of election and demand for sale is filed with the public trustee or the time the order of foreclosure is delivered to the sheriff a deposit of three hundred dollars, which shall be applied against the fee and expenses of the public trustee or sheriff described in this section.

Date of foreclosure sale.
Whenever property is to be sold by virtue of the foreclosure of any mortgage, deed of trust, or other lien, whether through the public trustee or through court, the date fixed for such sale shall be:

1. In the case of a sale by the public trustee, not less than forty-five days nor more than sixty days, or such longer period as provided in the deed of trust, after the date of recording of the notice of election and demand; and

2. In the case of a foreclosure through the court, not less than forty-five days after the date of commencement of the action to foreclose.

In case of a publication of an erroneous notice of sale in connection with a public trustee foreclosure, the sale may be postponed to a date subsequent to the expiration of the sixty-day period prescribed in subsection of this section but in no event to a date later than thirty days after the fifth correct publication of the corrected notice of sale.

Connecticut*

Connecticut is a Judicial State.
Connecticut has two distinct types of judicial foreclosures: Strict Foreclosure and Foreclosure by Sale.

Timeline
Day 150, Day 180, Day 30, Day 15, Day 90, Day 75, Day1

Judicial Foreclosure Steps
Lis Pendens is recorded and Complaint for Foreclosure is served on mortgagors and all parties claiming an interest in the property (defendants) at least 12 days before the Complaint is filed with the Court on the "Return Date" (Day 30). If the whereabouts of defendants cannot be determined, multiple newspaper publications may be required by the Court.

From Return Date, in-state defendants have 2 days to file an Appearance, out-of state defendants have 90 days unless actual knowledge of action can be proved. If Appearance is Pro-Se, defendant has 15 days to Answer.

If Appearance is by Counsel, defendant has 5 days to file a Disclosure of Defense following the filing of a Demand for Disclosure of Defense by the plaintiff. Several "waves" of Default Motions are usually required before they are all granted and the case claimed for judgment (Day 75).

Judgment of Strict Foreclosure is typically entered (Day 90) by the Court if there is no equity in the property above the debt being foreclosed.

There is no sale. The mortgagor is given a law date by which he must payoff the debt or loses his interest. All other defendants are also given law dates.

Upon failure of payment, title automatically vests in the foreclosing mortgagee on the "vesting date" (Day 150).

The period between judgment and the vesting date is the redemption period and is discretionary with the judge. Hardship cases may prolong the redemption period.

Judgment of Foreclosure by Sale is typically entered by the Court if there is equity in excess of the debt being foreclosed (or if there is a federal lien). The length of the redemption period between judgment and sale date varies in the discretion of the judge. Confirmation of Sale takes at least 30 days (Day 180).

Tenants whose identities are known and who are served at the onset of the foreclosure action may be ejected by obtaining an Order of Ejectment in the foreclosure action. Tenants whose identities are not known must be served in a separate Summary Process Action.

Deficiency Judgment for the difference between the total debt and the appraised value of the property may be obtained only if a Motion for Deficiency Judgment is filed within 30 days after title vests in the foreclosing mortgagee in a Strict Foreclosure. In a

Foreclosure by Sale, a deficiency judgment may similarly be obtained for the difference between the total debt and the net proceeds of Sale.

*Courtesy of National Foreclosure Professionals and Connecticut State Statutes

Delaware*

Delaware is a Judicial State.

Lenders in Delaware are given a number of options in which they may pursue judicial foreclosure, but the most commonly used procedure is the Scire Facias.

This proceeding is quite different from other judicial foreclosures because instead of the lender having to prove the borrower is in default of the mortgage, the borrower has to prove he isn't.

Although the suit to obtain an order for foreclosure is filed by the lender, the borrower must appear in court within twenty (20) days of being served a writ to provide evidence as to why the foreclosure should not take place.

Unless the court is satisfied with the borrowers explanation and evidence, they will authorize a foreclosure sale. Said sale must be conducted by the sheriff and held either at the courthouse or at the property itself at least fourteen (14) days after the notice of sale is posted on the property and in other public places throughout the county in which it is located.

The buyer has no right of redemption once the court has confirmed the sale.

*Courtesy of Delaware State Statutes

Florida*

Florida is a Judicial State Equity
All mortgages shall be foreclosed in equity. In a mortgage foreclosure action, the court shall sever for separate trial all counterclaims against the foreclosing mortgagee.

The foreclosure claim shall, if tried, be tried to the court without a jury.

Legal notice concerning foreclosure proceedings
Whenever a legal advertisement, publication, or notice relating to a foreclosure proceeding is required to be placed in a newspaper, it is the responsibility of

the petitioner or petitioner's attorney to place such advertisement, publication, or notice.
The advertisement, publication, or notice shall be placed directly by the attorney for the petitioner, by the petitioner if acting pro se, or by the clerk of the court.

Order to show cause; entry of final judgment of foreclosure; payment during foreclosure
(1) After a complaint in a foreclosure proceeding has been filed, the mortgagee may request an order to show cause for the entry of final judgment and the court shall immediately review the complaint.
If, upon examination of the complaint, the court finds that the complaint is verified and alleges a cause of action to foreclose on real property, the court shall promptly issue an order directed to the defendant to show cause why a final judgment of foreclosure should not be entered.

(A) The order shall:

1. Set the date and time for hearing on the order to show cause. However, the date for the hearing may not be set sooner than 20 days after the service of the order. When service is obtained by publication, the date for the hearing may not be set sooner than 30 days after the first publication.
The hearing must be held within 60 days after the

date of service. Failure to hold the hearing within such time does not affect the validity of the order to show cause or the jurisdiction of the court to issue subsequent orders.

2. Direct the time within which service of the order to show cause and the complaint must be made upon the defendant.

3. State that the filing of defenses by a motion or by a verified or sworn answer at or before the hearing to show cause constitutes cause for the court not to enter the attached final judgment.

4. State that the defendant has the right to file affidavits or other papers at the time of the hearing and may appear personally or by way of an attorney at the hearing.

5. State that, if the defendant files defenses by a motion, the hearing time may be used to hear the defendant's motion.

6. State that, if the defendant fails to appear at the hearing to show cause or fails to file defenses by a motion or by a verified or sworn answer or files an answer not contesting the foreclosure, the defendant may be considered to have waived the right to a hearing and in such case the court may enter a final judgment of foreclosure ordering the clerk of the court to conduct a foreclosure sale.

7. State that if the mortgage provides for reasonable

attorney's fees and the requested attorney's fees do not exceed 3 percent of the principal amount owed at the time of filing the complaint, it is unnecessary for the court to hold a hearing or adjudge the requested attorney's fees to be reasonable.

8. Attach the final judgment of foreclosure the court will enter, if the defendant waives the right to be heard at the hearing on the order to show cause.

9. Require the mortgagee to serve a copy of the order to show cause on the mortgagor in the following manner: If the mortgagor has been served with the complaint and original process, service of the order may be made in the manner provided in the Florida Rules of Civil Procedure.
If the mortgagor has not been served with the complaint and original process, the order to show cause, together with the summons and a copy of the complaint, shall be served on the mortgagor in the same manner as provided by law for original process. Any final judgment of foreclosure entered under this subsection is for in rem relief only.

Nothing in this subsection shall preclude the entry of a deficiency judgment where otherwise allowed by law.

(B) The right to be heard at the hearing to show cause is waived if the defendant, after being served as provided by law with an order to show cause, engages in conduct that clearly shows that the defendant has relinquished the right to be heard on that order.

The defendant's failure to file defenses by a motion or by a sworn or verified answer or to appear at the hearing duly scheduled on the order to show cause presumptively constitutes conduct that clearly shows that the defendant has relinquished the right to be heard. If a defendant files defenses by a motion or by a verified or sworn answer at or before the hearing, such action constitutes cause and precludes the entry of a final judgment at the hearing to show cause.

(C) In a mortgage foreclosure proceeding, when a default judgment has been entered against the mortgagor and the note or mortgage provides for the award of reasonable attorney's fees.

It is unnecessary for the court to hold a hearing or adjudge the requested attorney's fees to be reasonable if the fees do not exceed 3 percent of the principal amount owed on the note or mortgage at the time of filing, even if the note or mortgage does not specify the percentage of the original amount that would be paid as liquidated damages.

(D) If the court finds that the defendant has waived the right to be heard as provided in paragraph (b), the court shall promptly enter a final judgment of foreclosure.

If the court finds that the defendant has not waived the right to be heard on the order to show cause, the court shall then determine whether there is cause not to enter a final judgment of foreclosure. If the court finds that the defendant has not shown cause, the court shall promptly enter a judgment of foreclosure.

In an action for foreclosure, other than residential real estate, the mortgagee may request that the court enter an order directing the mortgagor defendant to show cause why an order to make payments during the pendency of the foreclosure proceedings or an order to vacate the premises should not be entered.

(A) The order shall:

1. Set the date and time for hearing on the order to show cause. However, the date for the hearing shall not be set sooner than 20 days after the service of the order. Where service is obtained by publication, the date for the hearing shall not be set sooner than 30 days after the first publication.

2. Direct the time within which service of the order to show cause and the complaint shall be made upon the defendant.

3. State that the defendant has the right to file affidavits or other papers at the time of the hearing and may appear personally or by way of an attorney at the hearing.

4. State that, if the defendant fails to appear at the hearing to show cause and fails to file defenses by a motion or by a verified or sworn answer, the defendant may be deemed to have waived the right to a hearing and in such case the court may enter an order to make payment or vacate the premises.

Require the mortgagee to serve a copy of the order to show cause on the mortgagor in the following manner:

If the mortgagor has been served with the complaint and original process, service of the order may be made in the manner provided in the Florida Rules of Civil Procedure.

If the mortgagor has not been served with the complaint and original process, the order to show cause, together with the summons and a copy of the complaint, shall be served on the mortgagor in the same manner as provided by law for original process.

(B) The right to be heard at the hearing to show cause is waived if the defendant, after being served as provided by law with an order to show cause, engages in conduct that clearly shows that the defendant has relinquished the right to be heard on that order.

The defendant's failure to file defenses by a motion or by a sworn or verified answer or to appear at the hearing duly scheduled on the order to show cause presumptively constitutes conduct that clearly shows that the defendant has relinquished the right to be heard,

(C) If the court finds that the defendant has waived the right to be heard, the court may promptly enter an order requiring payment in the amount provided in paragraph (f) or an order to vacate.

(D) If the court finds that the mortgagor has not waived the right to be heard on the order to show cause, the court shall, at the hearing on the order to show cause, consider the affidavits and other showings made by the parties appearing and make a determination of the probable validity of the underlying claim alleged against the mortgagor and the mortgagor's defenses.

If the court determines that the mortgagee is likely to prevail in the foreclosure action, the court shall enter an order requiring the mortgagor to make the payment described in paragraph

(E) the mortgagee and provide for a remedy as described in paragraph

(F). However, the order shall be stayed pending final adjudication of the claims of the parties if the mortgagor files with the court a written undertaking executed by a surety approved by the court in an amount equal to the unpaid balance of the mortgage on the property, including all principal, interest, unpaid taxes, and insurance premiums paid by the mortgagee.

In the event the court enters an order requiring the mortgagor to make payments to the mortgagee, payments shall be payable at such intervals and in such amounts provided for in the mortgage instrument before acceleration or maturity.

The obligation to make payments pursuant to any order entered under this subsection shall commence from the date of the motion filed hereunder. The order shall be served upon the mortgagor no later than 20 days before the date specified for the first payment.

The order may permit, but shall not require the

mortgagee to take all appropriate steps to secure the premises during the pendency of the foreclosure action.

In the event the court enters an order requiring payments the order shall also provide that the mortgagee shall be entitled to possession of the premises upon the failure of the mortgagor to make the payment required in the order unless at the hearing on the order to show cause the court finds good cause to order some other method of enforcement of its order.

All amounts paid pursuant to this section shall be credited against the mortgage obligation in accordance with the terms of the loan documents, provided, however, that any payments made under this section shall not constitute a cure of any default or a waiver or any other defense to the mortgage foreclosure action.

Upon the filing of an affidavit with the clerk that the premises have not been vacated pursuant to the court order, the clerk shall issue to the sheriff a writ for possession which shall be governed by the provisions

*Courtesy of Florida State Statutes
Georgia*

Georgia is a non-judicial state.
Send Pre-Acceleration Letter if not sent by client
The FNMA security instrument requires 30 days written notice to the borrower that the loan will be accelerated and foreclosure commenced. Usually this Letter is sent by the lender.

Send Acceleration/Demand Letter
This letter provides the borrower with 10 days in which to pay the entire debt without attorney fees being added pursuant to Georgia law and provides the borrower with a copy of the newspaper ad pursuant to Georgia law.

Send foreclosure ad to newspaper
Foreclosure ads must be published once a week for four weeks immediately preceding the foreclosure sale date.

Conduct foreclosure sale
Foreclosure sales may be held only on the first Tuesday of the month unless that day is New Years Day or July 4 in which event; foreclosures are conducted on the following day. The foreclosures must be conducted between 10:00 a.m. and 4:00 p.m.

File eviction if necessary
Eviction is judicial and generally takes about 30 days
*Courtesy of National Foreclosure Professionals and Georgia State Statutes

Hawaii*

Hawaii-Judicial State
Filing a complaint

The process begins with a demand letter. If default is not cured, a complaint is filed along with a notice of pendency of action. The mortgagor has 21 days to respond to the complaint or its automatic foreclosure.

Notice of Sale
The notice of intent to foreclose must be published once a week for 3 consecutive weeks, the last publication cannot be less than 14 days before the day of sale, in a newspaper having a general circulation in the county in which the property is located. Notice must be posted on the premises not less than 21 days before the day of sale. Notice must state:

The date, time, and place of the public sale, the description of the property, including the address, the name of the mortgagor and the borrower, the name of the lender, the amount owed on the property, the name of the trustee conducting the public sale, and the terms and conditions of the public sale.

Cure loan time
Up until 3 days before the sale, the borrower may cure the loan and stop the sale by paying the debt, costs, and fees, incurred through the foreclosure process.
*Courtesy of Hawaii State Statutes

Idaho*

Idaho is a Non-Judicial State
MANNER OF FORECLOSURE --NOTICE --SALE

A trust deed may be foreclosed subsequent to recording notice of default as hereinbefore provided, and at least one hundred twenty (120) days before the day fixed by the trustee for the trustee's sale, notice of such sale shall be given by registered or certified mail, return receipt requested, to the last known address of the following persons or their legal representatives, if any: **The notice of sale shall set forth:**

1) The names of the grantor, trustee and beneficiary in the trust deed.

2) A description of the property covered by the trust deed.

3)The book and page of the mortgage records or the recorder's instrument number where the trust deed is recorded.

4) The default for which the foreclosure is made.

5) The sum owing on the obligation secured by the trust deed.

6)The date, time and place of the sale which shall be held at a designated time after 9:00 a.m. and before 4:00 p.m., Standard Time, and at a designated place in the county or one of the counties where the property is located.

At least three(3)good faith attempts shall be made on different days over a period of not less than seven (7) days each of which attempts must be made at least thirty (30) days prior to the day of the sale to serve a copy of the notice of sale upon an adult occupant of the real property in the manner in which a summons is served.

At the time of each such attempt, a copy of the notice of sale shall be posted in a conspicuous place on the real property unless the copy of the notice of sale previously posted remains conspicuously posted. Provided, however, that if during such an attempt personal service is made upon an adult occupant and a copy of the notice is posted, then no further attempt at personal service and no further posting shall be required.

Provided, further, that if the adult occupant personally served is a person to whom the notice of sale was required to be mailed (and was mailed) pursuant to the foregoing subsections of this section, then no posting of the notice of sale shall be required.
A copy of the notice of sale shall be published in a newspaper of general circulation in each of the counties in which the property is situated once a week for four (4) successive weeks, making four (4) publishing's in all, with the last publication to be at least thirty (30) days prior to
the day of sale.
An affidavit of mailing notice of sale and an affidavit of posting (when required) and publication of notice of sale shall be recorded in the mortgage records in the counties in which the property described in the deed is situated at least twenty (20) days prior to the date of sale.

The sale shall be held on the date and at the time and place designated in the notice of sale. The trustee shall sell the property in one parcel or in separate parcels at auction to the highest bidder. Any person, including the beneficiary under the trust deed, may bid at the trustee's sale. The attorney for such trustee may conduct the sale and act in such sale as the auctioneer of trustee.

The trustee may postpone the sale of the property upon request of the beneficiary by publicly announcing at the time and place originally fixed for the sale, the postponement to a stated subsequent date and hour.
No sale may be postponed to a date more than thirty (30) days subsequent to the date from which the sale is postponed. A postponed sale may itself be postponed in the same manner and within the same time limitations as provided in this subsection.

The purchaser at the sale shall forthwith pay the price bid and upon receipt of payment the trustee shall execute and deliver the trustee's deed to such purchaser, provided that in the event of any refusal to pay purchase money, the officer making such sale shall have the right to resell or reject any subsequent bid as provided by law in the case of sales under execution.

The trustee's deed shall convey to the purchaser the interest in the property which the grantor had, or had the power to convey, at the time of the execution by him of the trust deed together with any interest the grantor or his successors in interest acquired after the execution of such trust deed.

The purchaser at the trustee's sale shall be entitled to possession of the property on the tenth day following the sale, and any persons remaining in possession thereafter under any interest except one prior to the deed of trust shall be deemed to be tenants at sufferance.

Whenever all or a portion of any obligation secured by a deed of trust which has become due by reason of a default of any part of that obligation, including taxes, assessments, premiums for insurance or advances made by a beneficiary in accordance with the terms of the deed of trust, the grantor or his successor in interest in the trust property or any part thereof, or any beneficiary under a subordinate deed of trust.

Or any person having a subordinate lien or encumbrance of
record thereon, at any time within one hundred fifteen (115) days of the recording of the notice of default under such deed of trust, if the power of sale therein is to be exercised, or otherwise at any time prior to the entry of a decree of foreclosure, may pay to the beneficiary or their successors in interest, respectively, the entire amount then due under the terms of the deed of trust and the obligation secured.
*Courtesy of Idaho State Statutes

Illinois*

Illinois is a Judicial State
Notice of Judgment
At least 30 days prior to the entry of a judgment of foreclosure, any person identified in the affidavit shall be given a notice of the foreclosure.

A notice of foreclosure, whether the foreclosure is initiated by complaint or counterclaim, shall be constructive notice of the pendency of the foreclosure to every person claiming an interest in or lien on the mortgaged real estate, whose interest or lien has not been recorded prior to the recording of such notice of foreclosure.

Such notice of foreclosure must be executed by any party or any party's attorney and shall include the names of all plaintiffs and the case number, the court in which the action was brought, the names of title holders of record, a legal description of the real estate sufficient to identify it with reasonable certainty, a common address or description of the location of the real estate and identification of the mortgage sought to be foreclosed.

Notice of Sale.
The notice of sale shall include at least the following information,:

The name, address and telephone number of the person to contact for information regarding the real estate, the address of the property, a legal description of the property, a description of the improvements, the time and place of sale, the times specified in the judgment, the case title, number, and court which the foreclosure was filed, and terms of the sale.

The notice of sale shall be published at least 3 consecutive calendar weeks (Sunday through Saturday), once in each week, the first such notice to be published not more than 45 days prior to the sale, the last such notice to be published not less than 7 days prior to the sale, by:
(A) advertisements in a newspaper circulated to the general public in the county in which the real estate is located, in the section of that newspaper where legal notices are commonly placed and (6) separate advertisements in the section of such a newspaper, which (except in counties with a population in excess of 3,000,000) may be the same newspaper, in which real estate other than real estate being sold as part of legal proceedings is commonly advertised to the general public; provided, that the separate advertisements in the real estate section need not include a legal description and that where both advertisements could be published in the same newspaper and that newspaper does not have separate legal notices and real estate advertisement sections, a single advertisement with the legal description shall be sufficient; and (ii) such other publications
as may be further ordered by the court.

The party who gives notice of public sale shall also give notice to all parties in the action who have appeared and have not theretofore been found by the court to be in default for failure to plead.

Such notice shall be given in the manner provided in the applicable rules of court for service of papers other than process and complaint, not more than 45 days nor less than 7 days prior to the day of sale.

After notice is given as required in this Section a copy thereof shall be filed in the office of the clerk of the court entering the judgment, together with a certificate of counselor other proof that notice has been served in compliance with this Section.

Notice of the sale may be given prior to the expiration of any reinstatement period or redemption period. No other notice by publication or posting shall be necessary unless required by order or rule of the court.

The person named in the notice of sale to be (e) Receipt upon Sale. Upon and at the sale of mortgaged real estate, the person conducting the sale shall give to the purchaser a receipt of sale.

The receipt shall describe the real estate purchased and shall show the amount bid, the amount paid, the total amount paid to date and the amount still to be paid therefore. An additional receipt shall be given at the time of each subsequent payment.

Certificate of Sale.

Upon payment in full of the amount bid, the person conducting the sale shall issue, in duplicate, and give to the purchaser a Certificate of Sale.

The Certificate of Sale shall be in a recordable form, describe the real estate purchased, indicate the date and place of sale and show the amount paid therefore. The Certificate of Sale shall further indicate

that it is subject
to confirmation by the court.
The duplicate certificate may be recorded in accordance with Section 12-121. The Certificate of Sale shall be freely assignable by endorsement thereon. Interest after Sale.

Any bid at sale shall be deemed to include, without the necessity of a court order, interest at the statutory judgment rate on any unpaid portion of the sale price from the date of sale to the date of payment.
*Courtesy of Illinois State Statutes

Indiana*

Indiana is a Judicial State
Judgment Rendered
If the court finds that the mortgaged real estate is residential real estate and has been abandoned, a judgment or decree of sale may be executed on the date the judgment of foreclosure or decree of sale is entered, regardless of the date the mortgage is executed.
A judgment and decree in a proceeding to foreclose a mortgage that is entered by a court having jurisdiction may be filed with the clerk in any county. After the period set forth expires, a person who may enforce the judgment and decree may file a praecipe with the clerk in any county where the judgment and decree is filed, and the clerk shall promptly issue and certify to the sheriff of that county a copy of the judgment and decree under the seal of the court.
Upon receiving a certified judgment, the sheriff shall,

sell the mortgaged premises or as much of the mortgaged premises as necessary to satisfy the judgment, interest, and costs at public auction at the office of the sheriff or at another location that is reasonably likely to attract higher competitive bids. The sheriff shall schedule the date and time of the sheriff's sale for a time certain between the hours of 10 a.m. and 4 p.m. on any day of the week except Sunday.

Notice of Sale
Before selling mortgaged property, the sheriff must advertise the sale by publication once each week for three (3) successive weeks in a daily or weekly newspaper of general circulation. The sheriff shall publish the advertisement in at least one (1) newspaper published and circulated in each county where the real estate is situated.

The first publication shall be made at least thirty (30) days before the date of sale. At the time of placing the first advertisement by publication, the sheriff shall also serve a copy of the written or printed notice of sale upon each owner of the real estate.
Service of the written notice shall be made as provided in the Indiana Rules of Trial Procedure governing service of process upon a person. The sheriff shall charge a fee of ten
dollars ($10) to one (1) owner and three dollars ($3) to each additional owner for service of written notice under this subsection. The fee is:
(1) a cost of the proceeding;
(2) to be collected as other costs of the proceeding

are collected; and

(3) to be deposited in the county general fund for appropriation for operating expenses of the sheriff's department.

The sheriff also shall post written or printed notices of the sale in at least three (3) public places in each township in which the real estate is situated and at the door of the courthouse of each county in which the real estate is located.

If the sheriff is unable to procure the publication of a notice within the county, the sheriff may dispense with publication. However, the sheriff shall state that the sheriff was not able to procure the publication and explain the reason why publication was not possible.

Sheriff's sale

A sheriff shall offer to sell and sell property on foreclosure in a manner that is reasonably likely to bring the highest net proceeds from the sale after deducting the expenses of the offer and sale.

*Courtesy of Indiana State Statutes
Iowa*

Iowa is a Judicial State

They file a petition and application for a receiver. The delinquent homeowner has 21 days to file an answer. There is a hearing on the motion of judgment, the ruling on the motion, and finally the execution.

Notice of Sale

Notice of the sale must be posted in at least three

public places of the county, one of which shall be at the county courthouse. In addition, there shall be two weekly publications of such notice in a local newspaper printed in the county, with the first publication being at least four weeks before the date of sale, and the second publication a least one week before the date of sale.

If the borrower occupies the property, the notice must be served to them at least twenty days prior to the date of the sale.

Notice of sale shall include time, date and place of sale. The sale must occur at public auction, between 9:00 am and 4:00 pm and the time must be stated clearly in the notice of sale. The sheriff shall receive and give a receipt for a sealed written bid submitted prior to the public auction.

The sheriff may require all sealed written bids to be accompanied by payment. The sheriff must keep all written bids sealed until the commencement of the public auction, at which time the sheriff will open and announce the written bids.

*Courtesy of Iowa State Statutes

Kansas*

Kansas is a Judicial State

A lawsuit is filed to obtain a court order to foreclose. Upon receiving all claims, the court will make a judgment in favor of the lender and against the borrower for the balance due. The sheriff is directed to auction off the property to the highest bidder.

The notice of the time and sale must be advertised once a week for three (3) consecutive weeks, with the last publication being no more than fourteen (14) and no less than seven (7) days before the borrower scheduled date of sale. Notice of the sale must also be sent to the within five (5) days of the first advertisement

Unless otherwise ordered by the court, the sale is held at the courthouse in the county where the property resides. The sale is by public auction to the highest bidder, who will receive a certificate of purchase.
After the sale is confirmed, the winning bidder will be entitled to receive a sheriff's deed once the borrowers right of redemption has expired.
The borrower typically has twelve (12) months from the date of the foreclosure sale to redeem the property.
*Courtesy of Kansas State Statutes

Kentucky*

Kentucky is a Judicial State
The complaint initiating a foreclosure action must be filed in a circuit court where the property is located. There is a filing of lis pendens. The notice of action is filed, and is sent to the defendant who obviously has an opportunity of respond, 21 days to be exact from the date of service. If no response, the plaintiff can move for a default judgment.
A motion is then made for judgment. The judgment may be default judgment, summary judgment, or agreed judgment. Entry of judgment occurs, followed by advertising of sale.

Notice of Sale

Advertising of sale occurs once a week for 3 straight weeks in a newspaper and must state the sum of money for which the sale is to be made. The property is sold on the courthouse steps.

Redemption Period

Seller has 12 months to redeem the property by paying the amount for which the property was sold, plus interest.

*Courtesy of Kentucky State Statutes

Louisiana*

Louisiana is a Judicial State

A suit is filed seeking a judgment for the debt due and recognizing the mortgage or security interest. If an answer is not timely filed, a default judgment is possible.

If a default judgment cannot be obtained, a motion for summary judgment is frequently sought. Once a final judgment is obtained, the property can be sold. The property is sold in a sheriff's sale.

Deposit

A deposit of 10 percent of the sale price is required down, the balance within 30 days or the property is resold and the successful bidder looses the deposit.

Time Frame

The time frame to complete a Louisiana foreclosure varies from case to case and from court to court. In general, one can expect a Louisiana foreclosure to be

completed in three to five months unless delayed by events that cannot be controlled, such as improper documentation, service of process problems, bankruptcy, injunction, and the like.
*Courtesy of Louisiana State Statutes

Maine*

Maine is a Judicial State
Commencement of foreclosure by civil action
The foreclosure must be commenced in accordance with the Maine Rules of Civil Procedure, and the mortgagee shall also record a copy of the complaint or a clerk's certificate of the filing of the complaint in each registry of deeds in which the mortgage deed is or by law ought to be recorded
and such recording thereafter constitutes record notice of commencement of foreclosure.

The complaint must allege with specificity the plaintiff's claim by mortgage on such real estate, describe the mortgaged premises intelligibly, state the existence of public utility easements, if any, that were recorded subsequent to the mortgage and prior to the commencement of the foreclosure proceeding and without mortgagee consent, state the amount due on the mortgage, state the condition broken and by reason of such breach demand a foreclosure and sale.

Service of process on all parties in interest and all proceedings must be in accordance with the Maine

Rules of Civil Procedure.

"Parties in interest" include mortgagors, holders of fee interest, mortgagees, lessees pursuant to recorded leases or memoranda thereof, lienors and attaching creditors all as reflected by the indices in the registry of deeds and the documents referred to therein affecting the mortgaged premises, through the time of the recording of the complaint or the clerk's certificate.

Failure to join any party in interest does not invalidate the action nor any subsequent proceedings as to those joined.

Failure of the mortgagee to join, as a party in interest, the holder of any public utility easement recorded subsequent to the mortgage and prior to commencement of foreclosure proceedings is deemed consent by the mortgagee to such easement. Any other party having a claim to the real estate whose claim is not recorded in the registry of deeds as of the time of recording of the copy of the complaint or the clerk's certificate need not be joined in the foreclosure action, and any such party has no claim against the real estate after completion of the foreclosure sale; provided that any such party may move to intervene in the action for the purpose of being added as a party in interest at any time prior to the entry of judgment.

Hearing and judgment
After hearing, the court shall determine whether there has been a breach of condition in the plaintiff's mortgage, the amount due thereon, including

reasonable attorney's fees and court costs, the order of priority and those amounts, if any, that may be due to other parties that may appear and whether any public utility easements held by a party in interest survive the proceedings.

If the court determines that such a breach exists, a judgment of foreclosure and sale shall issue providing that if the mortgagor, his successors, heirs and assigns do not pay the sum that the court adjudges to be due and payable, with interest within the period of redemption, the mortgagee shall proceed with a sale as provided.

If the mortgagor, his successors, heirs and assigns pay to the mortgagee the sum that the court adjudges to be due and payable to the mortgagee with interest within the period of redemption, then the mortgagee shall forthwith discharge the mortgage and file a dismissal of the action for foreclosure with the clerk of the court.

On mortgages executed prior to October 1, 1975, unless the mortgage contains language to the contrary, the period of redemption shall be one year from the date of the judgment.

On mortgages executed on or after October 1, 1975, the period of redemption shall be 90 days from the date of the judgment. In either case, the redemption period shall begin to run upon entry of the judgment of foreclosure, provided that no appeal is taken.

Sale following expiration of period of redemption

Upon expiration of the period of redemption, if the mortgagor, or the mortgagor's successors, heirs or assigns have not redeemed the mortgage, any remaining rights of the mortgagor to possession terminate, and the mortgagee shall cause notice of a public sale of the premises stating the time, place and terms of the sale to be published once in each of 3 successive weeks in a newspaper of general circulation in the county in which the premises are located.

The first publication is to be made not more than 90 days after the expiration of the period of redemption. The public sale must be held not less than 30 days nor more than 45 days after the first date of that publication and may be adjourned, for any time not exceeding 7 days and from time to time until a sale is made, by announcement to those present at each adjournment.

The mortgagee, in its sole discretion, may allow the mortgagor to redeem or reinstate the loan after the expiration of the period of redemption but before the public sale. The mortgagee may convey the property to the mortgagor or execute a waiver of foreclosure and all other rights of all other parties remain as if no foreclosure had been commenced. The mortgagee shall sell the premises to the highest bidder at the public sale and deliver a deed of that sale to the purchaser.

The deed conveys the premises free and clear of all interests of the parties in interest joined in the action.

The mortgagee or any other party in interest may bid at the public sale. If the mortgagee is the highest bidder at the public sale, there is no obligation to account for any surplus upon a subsequent sale by the mortgagee.

Any rights of the mortgagee to a deficiency claim against the
Mortgagors are limited to the amount established as of the date of the public sale. The date of the public sale is the date on which bids are received to establish the sales price, no matter when the sale is completed by the delivery of the deed to the highest bidder.

In foreclosures by civil action commenced on or after January 1, 1995, the mortgagee shall cause notice of the public sale to be mailed by ordinary mail to all parties who appeared in the foreclosure action or to their attorneys of record. The notice must be mailed no less than 30 calendar days before the date of sale.

Failure to provide notice of the public sale to any party who appeared does not affect the validity of the sale.
*Courtesy of Maine State Statutes

Maryland*

Maryland is a Judicial State
Before making the sale, the trustee authorized to make the sale, shall file in the court in which action is docketed a bond to the state of Maryland in an amount substantially equal to the mortgage

indebtedness.

Notice of Sale

A notice of sale must be published in a newspaper of general circulation in the county where the property resides at least once a week for three (3) successive weeks, with the first publication to be not less than fifteen (15) days prior to sale and the last publication to be not more than one week prior to sale.

The trustee also sends a notice of the sale to the last known address of the mortgagor, and the owner of the title of the property. The notice of sale must be sent by certified
and by registered mail, not more than thirty (30) days and not less than ten (10) days before the
date of the sale.

The sale must be conducted by the person authorized to make the sale (i.e. trustee, sheriff) and may take place immediately outside the courthouse entrance, on the property itself or the location advertised in the notice of sale, if different. The terms of the sale vary by process.

After Sale

After the sale, the trustee sends a report to the court. Upon filing the report, it is published in the newspaper stating the foreclosure sale will be ratified 30 days from the date of notice.
*Courtesy of Maryland State Statutes

Massachusetts*

Massachusetts is a Non-Judicial State

Foreclosure under power of sale; procedure; notice; form

The mortgagee or person having his estate in the land mortgaged, or a person authorized by the power of sale, or the attorney duly authorized by a writing under seal, or the legal guardian or conservator of such mortgagee or person acting in the name of such mortgagee or person, may,

upon breach of condition and without action, do all the acts authorized or required by the power.

But, no sale under such power shall be effectual to foreclose a mortgage, unless, previous to such sale, notice thereof has been published once in each of three successive weeks, the first publication to be not less than twenty-one days before the day of sale, in a newspaper.

If any, published in the town where the land lies or in a newspaper with general circulation in the town where the land lies and notice thereof has been sent by registered mail to the owner or owners of record of the equity of redemption as of thirty days prior to the date of sale, said notice to be mailed at least fourteen days prior to the date of sale to said owner or owners to the address set forth in section sixty-one of chapter one hundred and eighty-five.

If the land is then registered or, in the case of unregistered land, to the last address of the owner or owners of the equity of redemption appearing on the records of the holder of the mortgage, if any, or if none, to the address of the owner or owners as given on his deed or on the petition for probate by which he acquired title, if any, or if in either case no address appears, then to the address to which the tax collector last sent the tax bill for the mortgaged premises to be sold, or if no tax bill has been sent for the last preceding three years, then to the address of any of the parcels of property in the name of said owner of record which are to be sold under the power of sale and unless a copy of said notice of sale has been sent by registered mail to all persons of record as of thirty days prior to the date of sale holding an interest in the property junior to the mortgage being foreclosed, said notice to be mailed at least fourteen days prior to the date of sale to each such person at the address of such person set forth in any document evidencing the interest or to the last address of such person known to the mortgagee.

Any person of record as of thirty days prior to the date of sale holding an interest in the property junior to the mortgage being foreclosed may waive at any time, whether prior or subsequent to the date of sale, the right to receive notice by mail to such person under this section and such waiver shall be deemed to constitute compliance with such notice requirement for all purposes.

If no newspaper is published in such town, or if there is no newspaper with general circulation in the town where the land lies, notice may be published in a newspaper published in the county where the land lies, and this provision shall be implied in every power of sale mortgage in which it is not expressly set forth.

A newspaper which by its title page purports to be printed or published in such town, city or county, and having a circulation therein, shall be sufficient for the purpose.

Notice of intention to foreclose, notice and affidavit

No action for a deficiency shall be brought after June thirtieth, nineteen hundred and forty-six by the holder of a mortgage note or other obligation secured by mortgage of real estate after a foreclosure sale by him taking place after January first, nineteen hundred and forty-six unless a notice in writing of the mortgagee's intention to foreclose the mortgage has been mailed, postage prepaid, by registered mail with return receipt requested, to the defendant sought to be charged with the deficiency at his last address then known to the mortgagee.

Together with a warning of liability for the deficiency, in substantially the form below, not less than twenty-one days before the date of the sale under the power in the mortgage, and an affidavit has been signed and sworn to, within thirty days after the foreclosure sale, of the mailing of such notice.

A notice mailed as aforesaid shall be a sufficient notice, and such an affidavit made within the time specified shall be prima facie evidence in such action of the mailing of such notice.

Notice of Sale

Notice of the foreclosure must be published once a week for three weeks in a newspaper of general circulation in the town where the land is located. The first publication must be at least 21 days before sale. Notice must also be sent by registered mail to any owner whose interest was recorded as of 30 days prior to the sale. The actual date of mailing must be at least 14 days prior to the foreclosure sale.

Persons authorized to redeem

The mortgagor or person claiming or holding under him may, after breach of condition, redeem the land mortgaged, unless the mortgagee, or person claiming or holding under him, has obtained possession of the land for breach of condition and has continued that possession for three years, or unless the land has been sold pursuant to a power of sale contained in the mortgage deed.

Right of redemption

Section 35. If, after the foreclosure of a mortgage not containing a power of sale, the person entitled to the debt recovers judgment for any part thereof on the ground that the value of the land mortgaged at the time of the foreclosure was less than the amount due, such recovery shall open the foreclosure.

And the person entitled may redeem the land although the three years limited therefore have expired, if suit for redemption is brought within one year after the recovery of such judgment.
*Courtesy of Massachusetts State Statutes

Michigan*

Michigan is a Foreclosure by Advertisement State
Mortgage Foreclosure by Advertisement:

1) A mortgage must include a Power of Sale that permits the property to be sold by public auction in the event of a default by the mortgagor in the terms and conditions of the mortgage.

2) All assignments of the mortgage must be recorded.

3) There must be a default under the terms of the mortgage, which makes the power of sale operative.

4) The mortgagor must be given any required notices of default provided for under the terms of the mortgage and Note.

5) The indebtedness must be accelerated.

6) There cannot be any judicial action pending at law for recovery of the debt or any portion thereof.

Publication and Posting Requirements:

1. A Notice of Sale is published in the newspaper. The Notice of Sale must include the following:

a. The names of the mortgagor and of the mortgagee, and the assignees of the mortgage, if any;

b. The date of the mortgage, and when recorded

c. The amount claimed due as of the date of the notice (the   date of the first publication).

d. The legal description of the property.

e. The length of the redemption period.

2. The Notice of Sale must be published for 4 successive weeks, at least once each week.

3. Within 15 days after the first publication a true copy

of the Notice must be posted in a conspicuous place on the property.

Foreclosure Sale:
The mortgagee may make a credit bid at the sale and purchase the property. The purchaser at the sale receives a Deed to the property.
The Deed only becomes operative if the property is not redeemed during the statutory redemption period.

Upon expiration of the statutory redemption period, the purchaser acquires all right, title and interest, which the mortgagor held at the time that the mortgage was executed, as well as any right, title or interest acquired by the mortgagor subsequent to the execution of the mortgage.

The mortgagor continues to have the right to possession of the property until after the expiration of the statutory redemption period.

The Sheriff's Deed should be recorded within 20 days of the date of sale. If the Deed is not recorded within 20 days of the date of sale, it does not invalidate the sale; however, the redemption period does not begin to run until the date the deed is recorded.

Statutory Redemption Period:
1. For a mortgage on residential property not exceeding 4 units and not more than 3 acres in size, if the amount claimed to be due on the mortgage at the date of the notice of foreclosure is more than 66-2/3% of the original indebtedness secured by the mortgage, the redemption period is 6 months.

2. If the property is abandoned as determined pursuant to the statute, the redemption period can be shortened to 30 days.

3. In any other case, the redemption period is 1 year from the date of sale.

4. The redemption price is an amount equal to the amount bid at the sale together with interest from the time of the sale, at the rate set forth in the mortgage.

Paying of Taxes or Insurance During the Redemption Period:
If after the foreclosure sale the purchaser pays taxes or hazard insurance on the property, that amount is added to the redemption amount, so long as an affidavit is recorded.

Redemption:
A purchaser's Deed is void if the mortgagor redeems the entire premises sold by paying the amount required within the applicable time limit. Payment must be made to the purchaser or the county register of deeds.

Eviction:
1. If the mortgagor does not redeem, and does not vacate the property, a summary proceedings action (eviction action) must be commenced in the district court.

2. A complaint is filed with the district court and the

occupants served.

3. A court date is held, usually within 10 to 20 days.

4. The former owners and any occupants are allowed 10 days from the date of the hearing (if a judgment is entered), to move from the premises (unless allowed more time by the mortgage company or its representative).

5. If the former owner does not vacate by the required date, a Writ of Restitution is filed with the court and issued by the judge.

6. A court officer goes out to the house and puts the mortgage company back into peaceful possession of the property by evicting the occupants and their possessions.

Sending of a Notice of Default Letter (if required under the mortgage) -30 days
Publication -The notice of a foreclosure sale must be published once a week for four weeks in a newspaper of general circulation in the county where the land is situated.

Within **15** days after the first publication, a true copy of the foreclosure notice must be posted in a conspicuous place on the premises described in the foreclosure notice. (with the sale taking place approximately 1 week after the end of publication (35 days).

The sale must be a public sale, conducted between the hours of 9 o'clock "in the forenoon" and 4 o'clock in the afternoon.

Redemption period -Six months (in some instances it could be 1 year).

Eviction -30 days.

*Courtesy of Michigan State Statutes

Minnesota*

Minnesota is a Non-Judicial State Non- Judicial Foreclosure:

Thirty-day demand letter must be sent on conventional loans prior to commencement of foreclosure.

Minnesota provides for non-judicial foreclosure when the mortgage deed contains a power of sale. A Power of Attorney authorizing an attorney to conduct the foreclosure along with a notice of pendency of the foreclosure must be filed of record prior to the commencement of foreclosure action. The Notice of Mortgage Foreclosure Sale must be published for six weeks. The Notice of Mortgage Foreclosure Sale must be served on the occupants of the mortgaged premises at least four weeks prior to the mortgage foreclosure sale. Junior lien holders and parties with an interest in the property may file a request for l'Jotice of Mortgage Foreclosure Proceeding. Notice is served on any requesting party by mail. Foreclosure sales are conducted by the Sheriff of the county where the property is located. The Sheriff issues a Certificate of Sale to the successful bidder. Outside bidder's must have cash or certified funds sufficient to outbid the foreclosing lender.

The foreclosure is subject to a statutory redemption period of six months. In a limited number of circumstances there is a twelve month redemption period. The twelve month period applies when the amount due as of the date of the Notice of Foreclosure Sale is less than 2(3 of the original principal amount; the mortgage premises exceed 10 acres in size with additional limitation; or the mortgage premises exceeds 40 acres in size. For mortgages executed after December 31, 1989 a court order may be obtained which reduces the redemption period to five weeks if the property has been abandoned.

During the redemption period an affidavit must be filed which details expenses advanced during the redemption period for taxes, insurance, and property preservation. The advances may not be collectable if the affidavit is not filed at least ten days prior to the expiration of redemption.

Judicial Foreclosure:
In order to obtain a deficiency judgment, the mortgage must be foreclosed by judicial action. Judicial foreclosure can also be used to cure title defects or if in a Foreclosure by Advertisement the occupants of the property are avoiding service. This involves the filing and service of a summons and complaint and obtaining a judgment. After judgment has been entered, the matter is scheduled for a judgment

139

and decree sale with the Sheriff. The Notice of Sheriff's Sale under judgment and decree must be published and posted for six weeks. The difference between the amount of the debt and the bid will establish the deficiency. After completion of the sale, the court must confirm the sale
results. Redemption will run from the date of confirmation. Collection of the deficiency can be commenced after confirmation of the sale.
*Courtesy of National Foreclosure Professionals and Minnesota State Statutes

Mississippi*
Mississippi is a Judicial and Non-Judicial State. The most common method used is Non-Judicial.

Mortgages and deeds of trust on land; to be referred to in deed of conveyance under foreclosure proceedings.

If there shall be a foreclosure and sale under any such mortgage or deed of trust on land, the deed of conveyance made to a purchaser pursuant to a sale there under shall recite the names of all parties to and the date of such mortgage or deed of trust, and also the book and page of the
record thereof, and if made by a substituted trustee shall also recite the book and page of the record of his substitution and appointment; but the omission of such recitations shall not invalidate the deed of conveyance.

How lands sold under mortgages and deeds in trust

All lands comprising a single tract, and wholly described by the subdivisions of the governmental surveys, sold under mortgages and deeds of trust, shall be sold in the manner provided by section one hundred eleven of the constitution for the sale of lands in pursuance of a decree of court, or under execution. All lands sold at public outcry under deeds of trust or other contracts shall be sold in the county in which the land is located, or in the county of the residence of the grantor, or one of the grantors in the trust deed, provided that where the land is situated in two or more counties, the parties may contract for a sale of the whole in any of the counties in which any part of the land lies. Sale of said lands shall be advertised for three consecutive weeks preceding such sale, in a newspaper published in the county, or, if none is so published, in some paper having a general circulation therein, and by posting one notice at the courthouse of the county where the land is situated, for said time, and such notice and advertisement shall disclose the name of the original mortgagor or mortgagors in said deed of trust or other contract. No sale of lands under a deed of trust or mortgage, shall be valid unless such sale shall have been advertised as herein provided for, regardless of any contract to the contrary. An error in the mode of sale such as makes the sale void will not be cured by any statute of limitations, except as to the ten-year statute of adverse possession.

Deed of trust or mortgage; how sale made when terms not specified

If a deed of trust or mortgage, with a power of sale, be silent as to the place and terms of sale and mode of advertising, a sale may be made after condition broken, for cash, upon such notice, and at such time and place as is required for sheriff's sale of like property. But all such sales shall be made in the county where the land is located, or in the county of the residence of the grantor or one of the grantors, provided that where the land is situated in two or more counties, the parties may contract for a sale of the whole, or any part thereof, in either county in which a part of the land lies.

Accelerated debt may be reinstated by payment of all default before sale.

Where there is a series of notes or installment payments secured by a deed of trust, mortgage or other lien, and a provision is inserted in such instrument to secure them to the effect that upon a failure to pay anyone (1) note or installment, or the interest thereon, or any part thereof, or for failure to pay taxes or insurance premiums on the property described in such instrument and the subject of such lien, that all the debt secured thereby should become due and collectible, and for any such reason the entire indebtedness shall have been put in default or declared due, the debtor, or any interested party, may at any time before a sale be made under the terms and provisions of such instrument, or by virtue of such lien, stop a threatened sale under the powers contained in such instrument or stop any proceeding in any court to enforce such lien by paying the amount of the note or installment then due or past due by its terms, with all accrued costs, attorneys' fees and trustees' fees on the amount actually past due by the terms of such instrument or lien, rather than the amount accelerated, and such taxes or insurance premiums due and not paid, with proper interest thereon, if such should have been paid by any interested party to such instrument. Any such payment or payments shall reinstate, according to the terms of such instrument, the amount so accelerated, the same as if such amount not due by its terms had not been accelerated or put in default.

Deed of trust or mortgage; power of sale; relationship of trustee to other party to deed of trust; beneficiary may purchase at sale made under power of sale.
(1) A deed of trust or mortgage may be in the form of a conveyance, to the end, before the words "witness my signature," and then as follows, viz.: "In trust to secure (here state what is secured, and all the necessary provisions).
"Witness my signature, the _____day of_____, A. D. _____
Notwithstanding the form of conveyance, any deed of trust or mortgage which has been made or shall hereafter be made may confer on the trustee or mortgagee and their successors, assignees and

agents the power of sale. Furthermore, any person may be appointed and may perform the duties of the trustee in a deed of trust, and such person shall not be disqualified nor shall the acts of such person be invalid because of the relationship of such person to any other party to the deed of trust. The beneficiary of a deed of trust or the mortgagee of a mortgage may purchase at any sale which has been made or shall hereafter be made under a power of sale, and any such sale shall not be invalid because of the relationship of such person to any other
party to the deed of trust.

Sheriff's conveyance.
A conveyance of land sold by a sheriff under execution may be in the following form, and shall be sufficient to convey all of the title of the defendant in the execution, which any conveyance such officer might make would in such case convey; and a conveyance by a constable in like
form, the proper changes being made, shall have the like effect in case of sale made by him, viz.: "By virtue of an execution issued by the clerk of the circuit court of _____ county, on the day of , A.D. , returnable before said court on the Monday of , A.D. , to enforce the judgment of said court, rendered on the day of , A.D.
/ in favor of against , for dollars, and costs, I, as sheriff of   county, have this day, according to law, sold the following lands, to
wit: [here describe the land]; when became the best bidder therefore at the sum of dollars, and he having paid said sum of money, I now convey said land to

him.

"Witness my hand, the _____, A. D.

_____

_____Sheriff."
*Courtesy of Mississippi State Statutes
Missouri*

Missouri is a Non-Judicial State
Petition to foreclose.
All mortgagees of real estate or persons holding
security interests in personal estate, including
leasehold interests, when the debt or damages
secured amount to fifty dollars or more, may file a
petition in the office of the circuit court against the
mortgagor or the debtor and the actual tenants or
occupiers of the real estate, or persons in possession
of personal property, setting forth the substance of the
mortgage deed or security agreement, and praying
that judgment may be rendered for the debt or
damages, and that the equity of redemption may be
foreclosed, and the mortgaged property or collateral
sold to satisfy the amount due.

Where filed
If any part of the property be real estate, the petition
may be filed in any county where any part of the
mortgaged premises is situated; if it be exclusively
personal estate, it may be filed and proceeded with as
in other civil actions.

Mortgages and security agreements with power of

sale.

All mortgages of real property or security agreements providing for a security interest in personal property, or both, with powers of sale in the mortgagee or secured party, and all sales made by such mortgagee, secured party or his personal representatives, in pursuance of the provisions of the mortgages or security agreements, shall be valid and binding by the laws of this state upon the mortgagors and debtors, and all persons claiming under them, and shall forever foreclose all right and equity of redemption of the property so sold. Nothing herein shall be construed to affect in any way the rights of a tenant to the growing and harvested crops on lands foreclosed as aforesaid, to the extent of the interest of the tenant under the terms of contract or lease between the tenant and the mortgagor or his personal representatives.

Notice of Sale

All sales of real estate under a power of sale contained in any mortgage or deed of trust executed after August 28, 1989, shall be made in the county where the land to be sold is situated, and not less than twenty days' notice of such sale shall be given, whether so provided in such mortgage or deed of trust or not. Where the property to be sold is located in more than one county, the property may be sold in any county where a part of the property is located.

The notice shall set forth the date and book and page of the record of such mortgages or deeds of trust, the grantors, the time, terms and place of sale, and a

description of the property to be sold, and shall be given by advertisement, inserted for at least twenty times, and continued to the day of the sale, in some daily newspaper, in counties having cities of fifty thousand inhabitants or more, and in all other counties such notice shall be given by advertisement in
some weekly newspaper published in such county for four successive issues, the last insertion to be not more than one week prior to the day of sale, or in some daily, tri-weekly or semi-weekly paper published in such county at least once a week for four successive weeks. Such notice shall appear on the same day of each week, the last insertion to be not more than one week prior to the day of sale, and if there be no newspaper published in such county or city, such notice shall be published in the nearest newspaper thereto in this state. Nothing in this section shall be construed to authorize the giving of any shorter notice than that required by such mortgage or deed of trust. Where the property to be sold lies wholly or in part within the corporate limits of any city having or that may hereafter have a population of fifty thousand inhabitants or more, then the notice provided for in this section shall be published in a daily newspaper in such city and where the property to be sold lies wholly or in part within the corporate limits of a city extending into two or more counties, then the notice provided for in this section shall be published in some newspaper published in the county in which the property lies, in the manner provided in this
section for publication in such county, even though

such property may lie in a city having a population of fifty thousand inhabitants or more. Where the property to be sold is located in more than one county, the notices required in this section shall be published in each county in which a
part of the property is located. Other provisions of this section to the contrary notwithstanding, in any county of the first class not having a charter form of government and containing a portion of a city with a population over three hundred fifty thousand and in any county of the second class
containing a portion of a city with a population over three hundred fifty thousand, the notice requirements and this section may be met by advertisement in some weekly newspaper published in such counties for four successive issues, the last insertion to be not more than one week prior to the date of the sale.

Any person desiring notice of sale under any deed of trust or mortgage with power of sale upon real property may, at any time subsequent to recordation of such deed of trust or mortgage, cause to be filed for record in the office of the recorder of each county in which any part or parcel
of the real property is situated a duly acknowledged request for such notice of sale. This request shall specify the name and address of the person to whom the notice is to be bailed and shall identify the deed of trust or mortgage by stating the names of the parties thereto and the legal description of the land described therein and the book and page where the same is recorded or the recorder's number and shall be in substantially the following form:

"In accordance with RSMo, 443.325, request is hereby made that notice of sale under the deed of trust (or mortgage) recorded the....day of ,20..,(as recorder's number .... or in Book ...., Page ....) of the records of County, Missouri, the legal description of the property being .... in County, Missouri, executed by as Grantor (or Mortgagor) in which .... is named as beneficiary (or Mortgagee) and as Trustee, be mailed to .... (Name) at ...., (Address) ...., (City) (State). (Signature) (Acknowledgment)" A separate request shall be filed for each person desiring notice of sale.
 2. Upon the filing for record of such request, the recorder shall index the request in a separate index so that the name of the mortgagor or grantor shall be indexed as the grantor, and the name of the requesting party shall be indexed as the grantee.
3. In the event of foreclosure under a power of sale, the foreclosing mortgagee or trustee shall, not less than twenty days prior to the scheduled date of the sale, cause to be deposited in the United States mail an envelope certified or registered, and with postage prepaid, enclosing a
notice containing the information required in the published notice of sale addressed:

 (1) To each person whose name and address is set forth in any such request recorded at least forty days prior to the scheduled date of sale; and
(2) To the person shown by the records in the office of the recorder of deeds to be the owner of the property as of forty days prior to the scheduled date of foreclosure sale at the foreclosing mortgagee's last

known address for said record owner; and

(3) To the mortgagor or grantor named in the deed of trust or mortgage at the foreclosing mortgagee's last known address for said mortgagor or grantor.

(4) Actual receipt by the addressee of the envelope referred to above shall not be necessary to establish compliance with the notice requirements of subsection 3 hereof. Recording of receipt issued by the United States Post Office for certified or registered mail to evidence that said envelope has been delivered by the sender to the United States Post Office shall constitute proof of compliance with notice requirements of subsection 3 hereof.

4. The foreclosing mortgagee* or trustee of a deed of trust or mortgage filed subsequent to a deed of trust or mortgage for which a request has been recorded in accordance with subsection 1 hereof shall give notice to each person named in each such request so long as the prior deed of trust or mortgage identified in such notice has not been released of record.

5. The release of a deed of trust or mortgage shall cancel of record all requests for notice which pertain to the deed of trust or mortgage identified in such request.

Time of Sale

The trustee exercising a power of sale granted in any security instrument may in the trustee's discretion set the time for sale at any commercially reasonable time, unless the security instrument specifies an hour at which the sale is to occur. The time for sale will be deemed to be commercially reasonable if the sale is held between the hours of 9:00 a.m. and 5:00 p.m. on the date of sale. If no time is stated in the notice of sale, then the sale shall be held at the time customary for such sales in the county. If the trustee elects to state a specific time for sale in the notice of sale, then the sale shall be held at the time stated in the notice unless the sale is continued as may be otherwise provided by law.

Redemption before sale.
If such property is redeemed by payment to the officer before the sale, such officer shall make a certificate of such redemption, and acknowledge the same before some officer authorized to take acknowledgments of deeds for lands; and such certificate shall be recorded in the office in which the security instrument is recorded, and shall have the same effect as if a deed of release has been filed for record.

Foreclosures by trustee's sale
Deeds of trust in the nature of mortgages of lands may, in addition to being foreclosable by suit, be also foreclosed by trustee's sale at the option of the holder of the debt or obligation thereby secured and the mortgaged property sold by the trustee or his successor in the same manner and in all respects as in case of mortgages with power of sale; and all real estate which may be sold under any such power of sale in a mortgage deed of trust hereafter made and which at such sale shall be brought in by the holder of such debt or obligation or

by any other person for such holder
shall be subject to redemption by the grantor in such mortgage deed of trust or his heirs, devisees, executors, administrators, grantees or assigns at any time within one year from the date of the sale; provided, however, that such person so entitled to redeem shall give written notice at the sale or within ten days before the date advertised for the sale to the person making or who is to make the sale of the purpose to redeem if the sale and purchase are so made; and provided further, the said grantor, his representatives, grantees or assigns to make the redemption shall within the year pay the debt and interest or other obligation secured by such deed of trust and to accrue thereon together with all sums paid out by any holder thereof or purchaser at such sale or holder of the rights of such purchaser for interest and principal and either of any prior encumbrances, and for taxes and assessments and all legal charges and costs of the sale.

Redemption Period
No party shall have the right of redeeming from any such sale unless he shall have given the written notice specified in said section and shall within twenty days after such sale give
security to the satisfaction of the circuit court of the county in which the land is located for the payment of the interest on the debt or obligation secured by the mortgage deed of trust
under which the sale is made to accrue within such year after the sale is made, and for the payment in full of the legal charges and costs of the sale, and for the

payment of all interest accrued prior to the sale or thereafter which the purchaser at the sale or his representatives or assigns may pay on any prior encumbrance on the land, as well as the interest, which may accrue thereon during such year allowed for redemption whether so paid or not and all taxes and assessments and interest and costs thereon whether general or special accrued or accruing during such year allowed for redemption and whether paid by the purchaser at the sale or not together with interest at rate of six percent per annum on all sums so paid by the purchaser or those claiming under him and for damages for all waste committed or suffered by the party giving such security or those claiming under him during such year unless said property is so redeemed, and it shall be necessary to pay for such redemption all such sums to which the purchaser or those claiming under him should be entitled with interest as aforesaid. Said security shall be by bond executed by the person or persons so entitled to redeem with at least one good surety in a sum amply sufficient to cover the aggregate of all said sums exclusive of the principal debt or obligation, but including damages and interest, to be so absolutely paid
in event redemption is not made and the aggregate of all such shall be the measure of damages to be paid in satisfaction of said bond if such redemption is not made.

Certificate of sale
If the bond is given and approved the trustee at the purchaser's request shall execute, acknowledge and

deliver to him a certificate of sale or purchase giving a reference to the deed of trust, fact of sale and purchase. And if redemption is not made within the year as so provided

he shall thereupon execute to the purchaser or his heirs or devisees good and sufficient deed of conveyance upon the presentation of such certificate or showing of reason for its non-production to the satisfaction of the trustee. The rights, interests and estates of any of the parties may be conveyed by deed as interests in land are conveyed and trustee's deed may be made to the original purchaser and shall inure to his grantees. If the certificate of sale or any conveyance of

the purchaser's interest is recorded the purchaser and his grantee shall give a sufficient recordable acknowledgment of redemption if the same be made. Any prematurely executed

trustee's deed shall operate as a certificate of sale by the trustee, and if the trustee dies, becomes incapable or cannot be found the court may summarily and on ex parte application of the purchaser appoint a successor or commissioner to execute a good and sufficient

conveyance in completion of the trustee's sale if redemption be not made within the year provided. Both the certificate of sale and purchase and deed and the recitals therein shall each be prima facie evidence of the recitals therein.

*Courtesy of Missouri State Statutes

Montana*
Montana is a Judicial State
Trust indentures authorized --power of sale for breach in trustee.

(1) A transfer in trust of an interest in real property of an area not exceeding 40 acres may be made to secure the performance of an obligation of a grantor or any other person named in the indenture to a beneficiary. However, a trust indenture may not be substituted for a mortgage that was in existence on March 5, 1963.

(2) When a transfer in trust of an interest in real property is made to secure the performance of the obligation referred to in subsection (i), a power of sale is conferred upon the trustee to be exercised after a breach of the obligation for which the transfer is security.

(3) A trust indenture executed in conformity with this part may be foreclosed by advertisement and sale in the manner provided in this part or, at the option of the beneficiary, by judicial procedure as provided by law for the foreclosure of mortgages on real property. The power of sale may be exercised by the trustee without express provision in the trust indenture.

(4) If a trust indenture states that the real property involved does not exceed 40 acres, the statement is binding upon all parties and conclusive as to compliance with the provisions of this part relative to the power to make a transfer, trust, and power of sale.

Qualifications of trustee --successor trustee.

(1) The trustee of a trust indenture under this part must be:

(a) an attorney who is licensed to practice law in Montana;

(b) a bank, trust company, or savings and loan association authorized to do business in Montana under the laws of Montana or the United States; or

(c) a title insurer or title insurance producer or agency authorized to do business in Montana under the laws of Montana.

(2) The beneficiary may appoint a successor trustee at any time by filing for record, in the office of the clerk and recorder of each county in which the trust property or some part of the trust property is situated, a substitution of trustee. The substitution must identify the trust indenture by stating the names of the original parties to the trust indenture and the date of recordation and the book and page where the information is recorded, must state the name and mailing address of the new trustee, and must be executed and acknowledged by all of the beneficiaries designated in the trust indenture or their successors in interest. From the time the substitution is filed for record, the new trustee is vested with all the power, duties, authority, and title of the trustee named in the trust indenture and of any successor trustee.

Discontinuance of foreclosure proceedings when entire amount of default paid.

(1) Whenever all or a portion of any obligation secured by a trust indenture has, prior to the maturity date fixed in such obligation, become due or been declared due by reason of a breach or default in the performance of any obligation secured by the trust indenture, including a default in the payment of interest or of any installment of

principal or by reason of failure of the grantor to pay, in accordance with the terms of such trust indenture, taxes, assessments, premiums for insurance, or advances made by the beneficiary in accordance with the terms of such obligation
or of such trust indenture, the grantor or his successor in interest in the trust property or any part thereof or any other person having a subordinate lien or encumbrance of record thereon or any beneficiary under a subordinate trust indenture, at any time prior to the time fixed by the trustee
for the trustee's sale if the power of sale is to be exercised, may pay to the beneficiary or his successor in interest the entire amount then due under the terms of such trust indenture and the obligation secured thereby (including costs and expenses actually incurred and reasonable trustee's and attorney's fees) other than such portion of the principal as would not then be due had no default occurred and thereby cure the default theretofore existing.
(2) Thereupon all proceedings theretofore had or instituted to foreclose the trust indenture shall be canceled and the obligation and the trust indenture shall be reinstated and shall be and remain in force and effect the same as if no such acceleration had occurred.
(3) If the default is cured and the obligation and the trust indenture reinstated in the manner hereinabove provided, the beneficiary or his assignee shall, on demand of any person having an interest in the trust property, execute, acknowledge, and deliver to him a request that the trustee

execute, acknowledge, and deliver a cancellation of the recorded notice of sale under such trust indenture.

(4) Any beneficiary under a trust indenture or his assignee who, for a period of 30 days after such demand, refuses to request the trustee to execute, acknowledge, and deliver such cancellation shall be liable to the person entitled to such request for all damages resulting from such refusal.

(5) A cancellation of a recorded notice of sale shall, when executed and acknowledged, be entitled to be recorded and shall be sufficient if it sets forth a reference to the trust indenture and the book and page where the same is recorded, a reference to the notice of sale and to the

book and page where the same is recorded, and a statement that such notice of sale is canceled.

Conditions for foreclosure by advertisement and sale.

The trustee may foreclose a trust indenture by advertisement and sale under this part if:

(1) the trust indenture, any assignments of the trust indenture by the trustee or the beneficiary, and any appointment of a successor trustee are recorded in the office of the clerk and recorder of each county in which the property described in the trust indenture or some part thereof is Situated;

(2) there is a default by the grantor or other person owing an obligation or by their successors in interest, the performance of which is secured by the trust indenture, with respect to any provision in the indenture which authorizes sale in the event of default of such provision; and

(3) the trustee or beneficiary shall have filed for record in the office of the clerk and recorder in each county where the property described in the indenture or some part thereof is situated a notice of sale, duly executed and acknowledged by such trustee or beneficiary, setting forth:

(a) the names of the grantor, trustee, and beneficiary in the trust indenture and the name of any successor trustee;

(b) a description of the property covered by the trust indenture;

(c) the book and page of the mortgage records where the trust indenture is recorded;

(d) the default for which the foreclosure is made;

(e) the sum owing on the obligation secured by the trust indenture;

(f) the trustee's or beneficiary's election to sell the property to satisfy the obligation;

(g) the date of sale, which shall not be less than 120 days subsequent to the date on which the notice of sale is filed for record, and the time of sale, which shall be between the hours of 9 a.m. and 4 p.m., Mountain Standard Time;

(h) the place of sale which shall be at the courthouse of the county or one of the counties where the property is situated or at the location of the property or at the trustee's usual place of business if within the county or one of the counties where the property is situated.

Requests for copies of notice of sale.
At any time subsequent to the recordation of a trust indenture and prior to the recordation of notice of sale

under the indenture, any person desiring a copy of any notice of sale under a trust indenture (1) may cause to be filed for record in the office of the county clerk and recorder of the
county or counties in which any part or parcel of the real property is situated, a duly acknowledged request for a copy of any notice of sale, showing service upon the trustee. The
request shall contain the name and address of the person requesting a copy of the notice and shall identify the trust indenture by stating the names of the parties to the indenture, the date of recordation of the indenture, and the book and page where the indenture is recorded. The county
clerk and recorder shall immediately make a cross-reference of the request to the trust indenture either on the margin of the page where the trust indenture is recorded or in some other suitable place. No request, statement, or notation placed on the record pursuant to this section shall affect
title to the property or be deemed notice to any person that any person so recording the request has any right, title, interest in, lien, or charge upon the property referred to in the trust indenture.

Notice --sale --payment.
A trust deed may be foreclosed by advertisement and sale in the manner hereinafter provided:
(1) The trustee shall give notice of the sale in the following manner:
 (a) At least 120 days before the date fixed for the trustee's sale, a copy of the recorded notice of sale shall be mailed by registered or certified mail

to:

(i) the grantor, at the grantor's address as set forth in the trust indenture or (in the event no address of the grantor is set forth in the trust indenture) at the grantor's last known address;

(ii) each person designated in the trust indenture to receive notice of sale whose address is set forth therein, at such address;

(iii) each person who has filed for record a request for a copy of notice of sale within the time and in the manner hereinafter provided, at the address of such person as set forth in such request;

(iv) any successor in interest to the grantor whose interest and address appear of record at the filing date and time of the notice of sale, at such address;

(v) any person having a lien or interest subsequent to the interest of the trustee and whose lien or interest and address appear of record at the filing date and time of the notice of sale, at such address.

(b) At least 20 days before the date fixed for the trustee's sale, a copy of the recorded notice of sale shall be posted in some conspicuous place on the property to be sold. Upon request of the trustee, the notice of sale shall be posted by a sheriff or constable of the county wherein the property to be sold is located.

(c) A copy of the notice of sale shall be published in a newspaper of general circulation published in any county in which the property or some part thereof is situated, at least once each week for 3 successive weeks. If there is no such newspaper, then copies of the notice of sale shall be posted in at least three public places in each county in which the property or some part thereof is situated. The posting or the last publication shall be made at least 20 days before the date fixed for the trustee's sale.

(2) On or before the date of sale, there shall be recorded in the office of the clerk and recorder of each county where the property or some part thereof is situated, affidavits of mailing, posting, and publication showing compliance with the requirements of this section.

(3) On the date and at the time and place designated in the notice of sale, the trustee or his attorney shall sell the property at public auction to the highest bidder. The property may be sold in one parcel or in separate parcels, and any person, including the beneficiary under the trust indenture but excluding the trustee, may bid at the sale. The person making the sale may, for any cause he deems expedient, postpone the sale for a period not exceeding 15 days by public proclamation at the time and place fixed in the notice of sale. 1\10 other notice of the postponed sale need be given. In the event a sale cannot be held at the scheduled time by reason of the automatic stay provision of the United States Bankruptcy Code, 11 U.S.C. 362, or of a stay order issued by any court of competent jurisdiction, the person making the sale may, as often as he considers expedient, postpone the sale. Each postponement may not exceed 30 days, and all postponements, in the aggregate, may not exceed 120 days. Each postponement must be effected by a public proclamation at the time and

place fixed in the notice of sale or fixed by previous postponement. No other notice of the postponed sale need be given.

(4) The purchaser at the sale shall pay the price bid in cash, and upon receipt of payment, the trustee shall execute and deliver a trustee's deed to the purchaser. In the event the purchaser refuses to pay the purchase price, the person conducting the sale shall have the right to resell the
property at any time to the highest bidder. The party refusing to pay shall be liable for any loss occasioned thereby, and the person making the sale may also, in his discretion, thereafter reject any other bid of such person.

Disposition of proceeds of sale.
The trustee shall apply the proceeds of the trustee's sale as follows:
(1) to the costs and expenses of exercising the power of sale and of the sale, including
reasonable trustee's fees and attorney's fees;
 (2) to the obligation secured by the trust indenture;
 (3) the surplus, if any, to the person or persons legally entitled thereto, or the trustee, in his discretion, may deposit such surplus with the clerk and recorder of the county in
which the sale took place. Upon depositing such surplus, the trustee shall be discharged from all further responsibility therefore and the clerk and recorder shall deposit the same with the county treasurer subject to the order of the district court of

such county.

Deficiency judgment not allowed.

When a trust indenture executed in conformity with this part is foreclosed by advertisement and sale, no other or further action, suit, or proceedings shall be taken or judgment entered for any deficiency against the grantor or his surety, guarantor, or successor in interest, if any, on the note, bond, or other obligation secured by the trust indenture or against any other person obligated on such note, bond, or other obligation.

Trustee's deed. (1) The trustee's deed to the purchaser at the trustee's sale may contain, in addition to a description of the property conveyed, recitals of compliance with the requirements of this part relating to the exercise of the power of sale and the sale, including recitals of the facts concerning the default, the notice given, the conduct of the sale, and the receipt of the purchase money from the purchaser.

(2) When the trustee's deed is recorded in the deed records of the county or counties where the property described in the deed is situated, the recitals contained in the deed and in the affidavits

(2) shall be prima facie evidence in any court of the truth of the matters set forth therein, except that the same shall be conclusive evidence in favor of subsequent bona fide purchasers and encumbrancers for value and without notice.

(3) The trustee's deed shall operate to convey to the purchaser, without right of redemption, the trustee's

title and all right, title, interest, and claim of the grantor and his successors in interest and of all persons claiming by, through, or under them in and to the property sold, including all such right, title, interest, and claim in and to such property acquired by the grantor or his successors in interest subsequent to the execution of the trust indenture.

Possession.
The purchaser at the trustee's sale shall be entitled to possession of the property on the 10th day following the sale, and any persons remaining in possession after that date under any interest, except one prior to the trust indenture, shall be deemed to be tenants at will.
*Courtesy of Montana State Statutes

Nebraska*
Nebraska is a Judicial State
Power of sale conferred on trustee.
A power of sale may be conferred upon the trustee which the trustee may exercise and under which the trust property may be sold in the manner provided in the Nebraska Trust Deeds Act after a breach of an obligation for which the trust property is conveyed as security, or at the option of the beneficiary a trust deed may be foreclosed in the manner provided by law for the foreclosure of mortgages on real property. The power of sale shall be expressly provided for in the trust deed.

Sale of trust property; notice of default.
The power of sale herein conferred upon the trustee shall not be exercised until:
(l)The trustee shall first file for record in the office of the register of deeds of each county wherein the trust property or some part or parcel thereof is situated a notice of default identifying the trust deed by stating the name of the trustor named therein and giving the book and page or computer
system reference where the same is recorded and a description of the trust property, containing a statement that a breach of an obligation for which the trust property was conveyed as security has occurred, and setting forth the nature of such breach and of his or her election to sell or
cause to be sold such property to satisfy the obligation;
 (2) If the trust property is used in farming operations carried on by the trustor, not in any incorporated city or village, the notice of default also sets forth:
 (a) A statement that the default may be cured within two months of the filing for record of the notice of default and the obligation and trust deed may be thereby;

(b) A statement of the amount of the entire unpaid principal sum secured by the trust deed, the amount of interest accrued thereon to and including the date the notice of default is filed for record, and the dollar amount of the per diem interest accruing from and after such date;
and   (c) A statement of the amount of the unpaid principal which would not then be due had no

default occurred; and

(3) After the lapse of not less than one month, or two months if the notice of default is subject to subsection (2) of this section,

Sale of trust property
 (1) The trustee shall give written notice of the time and place of sale particularly describing the property to be sold by publication of such notice, at least five times, once a week for five consecutive weeks, the last publication to be at least ten days but not more than thirty days prior to the sale, in some newspaper haVing a general circulation in each county in which the property
to be sold, or some part thereof, is situated.

(2) The sale shall be held at the time and place designated in the notice of sale which shall be between the hours of nine a.m. and five p.m. and at the premises or at the courthouse of the county in which the property to be sold, or some part thereof, is situated.
(3) The notice of sale shall be sufficient if made in substantially the following form:

Notice of Trustee's Sale
 The following described property will be sold at public auction to the highest bidder at the door of the county courthouse in , County of , I\Nebraska, on , 19 .

Notice of default and sale
 (1) Any person desiring a copy of any notice of

default and of any notice of sale under any trust deed may, at any time subsequent to the filing for record of the trust deed and prior to the filing for record of a notice of default thereunder, file for record in the office of the register of deeds of any county in which any part or parcel of the trust property is situated a duly acknowledged request for a copy of any such notice of default and notice of sale. The request shall set forth the

name and address of the person or persons requesting copies of such notices and shall identify the trust deed by stating the names of the original parties thereto, the date of filing for record thereof, and the book and page or computer system reference where the same is recorded and shall be in substantially the following form: Request is hereby made that a copy of any notice of default and a copy of notice of sale under the trust deed filed for record , 19 , and recorded in book ...., page , (or computer system reference) Records of .. County, Nebraska, executed by as trustor, in which is named as beneficiary and... as trustee, be malled to (insert name)......at
.........(insert address) Signature .

(2) Not later than ten days after recordation of such notice of default, the trustee or beneficiary shall mail, by registered or certified mail with postage prepaid, a copy of such notice with the recording date shown thereon, addressed to each person whose name and address is set forth in a request therefore which has been recorded prior to the filing for record of the notice of default, directed to the address designated

in such request. At least twenty days before the date of sale, the trustee shall mail, by registered or certified mail with postage prepaid, a copy of the notice of the time and place of sale, addressed to each person whose name and address is set forth in a request therefore which has been recorded prior to the filing for record of the notice of
default, directed to the address designated in such request.

(3) Each trust deed shall contain a request that a copy of any notice of default and a copy of any notice of sale thereunder shall be mailed to each person who is a party thereto at the address of such person set forth therein, and a copy of any notice of default and of any notice of sale shall be mailed to each such person at the same time and in the same manner required as though a separate request therefore had been filed by each of such persons as provided in this section.

(4) If no address of the trustor is set forth in the trust deed and if no request for notice by such trustor has been recorded as provided in this section, a copy of the notice of default shall be published at least three times, once a week for three consecutive weeks, in a newspaper of general circulation in each county in which the trust property or some part thereof is situated, such publication to commence not later than ten days after the filing for record of the notice of default.
(5) No request for a copy of any notice filed for record pursuant to this section nor any statement or allegation in any such request nor any record thereof

shall affect the title to trust property or be deemed notice to any person that any person requesting copies of notice of default or of notice of sale has or claims any right, title, or interest in or lien or claim upon the trust property.

Sale of trust property

On the date and at the time and place designated in the notice of sale, the trustee shall sell the property at public auction to the highest bidder. The attorney for the trustee may conduct the sale. Any person, including the beneficiary, may bid at the sale. Every bid shall be deemed an irrevocable offer, and if the purchaser refuses to pay the amount bid by him for the property struck off to him at the sale, the trustee may again sell the property at any time to the highest bidder. The party refusing to pay shall be liable for any loss occasioned thereby and the trustee may also, in his discretion, thereafter reject any other bid of such person. The person conducting the sale may, for any cause he deems expedient, postpone the sale from time to time until it shall be completed and, in every such case, notice of postponement shall be given by public declaration thereof by such person at the time and place last appointed for the sale. No other notice of the postponed sale need be given unless the sale is postponed for longer than one day beyond the day designated in the notice of sale in which event notice thereof shall be given in the same manner as the original notice of sale is required to be given.

(1) The purchaser at the sale shall forthwith pay the price bid and upon receipt of payment the trustee shall execute and deliver his deed to such purchaser. The trustee's deed may contain recitals of compliance relating to the exercise of the power of sale and sale of the property described therein, including recitals concerning any mailing, personal delivery and publication of the notice of default, any mailing and the publication and posting of notice of sale, and the conduct of sale; and such recitals shall constitute prima facie evidence of such compliance and conclusive evidence thereof in favor of bona fide purchasers and encumbrancers for value and without notice.

(2) The trustee's deed shall operate to convey to the purchaser, without right of redemption, the trustee's title and all right, title, interest and claim of the trustor and his successors in interest and of all persons claiming by, through or under them, in and to the property sold, including all such right, title, interest and claim in and to such property acquired by the trustor or his successors in interest subsequent to the execution of the trust deed.
The trustee shall apply the proceeds of the trustee's sale, first, to the costs and expenses of exercising the power of sale and of the sale, including the payment of the trustee's fees actually incurred not to exceed the amount which may be provided for in the trust deed, second, to payment of the obligation secured by the trust deed, third, to the payment of junior trust deeds, mortgages, or other lien holders, and the balance, if any, to the person or persons legally

entitled
thereto.

Deficiency Judgment

At any time within three months after any sale of property under a trust deed, as hereinabove provided, an action may be commenced to recover the balance due upon the obligation for which the trust deed was given as security, and in such action the complaint shall set forth the entire amount of the indebtedness, which was secured by such trust deed and the amount for which such property was sold and the fair market value thereof at the date of sale, together with interest on such indebtedness from the date of sale, the costs and expenses of exercising the power of sale and of the sale. Before rendering judgment, the court shall find the fair market value at the date of sale of the property sold. The court shall not render judgment for more than the amount by which the amount of the indebtedness with interest and
the costs and expenses of sale, including trustee's fees, exceeds the fair market value of the property or interest therein sold as of the date of the sale, and in no event shall the amount of said judgment, exclusive of interest from the date of sale, exceed the difference between the amount for which the property was sold and the entire amount of the indebtedness secured thereby, including said costs and expenses of sale.
*Courtesy of Nebraska State Statutes

Nevada*
Nevada is a Non-Judicial State

A notice of default is recorded and elected to sell. A copy of the NOD and election to sell is mailed to the grantor and to the person who holds the title of record. A notice is then sent to the borrower declaring the entire balance due. After three months, If the borrower fails to cure the loan, then the property will be sold at foreclosure. The borrower has 35 days from the first day following the day on which the notice of default and election to sell was recorded to cure the
default.

Notice of Sale
The trustee must give notice of the time and place of sale at least 21 days before sale. The trustee must also post similar notices in three public places, and publish those notices three times in a newspaper once a week for three weeks.
Deficiency Judgment
There is a possibility the lender may sue for a deficiency within three months after the foreclosure sale, if proceeds from the sale failed to generate enough funds to payoff the
remaining balance.

Redemption Period
There is a one-year redemption on judicial sales.
*Courtesy of Nevada State Statutes

New Hampshire*
New Hampshire is a Non-Judicial State
This is a power of sale state. A "power of sale" is the

clause in a deed of trust or mortgage, in which the borrower pre-authorizes the sale of property to payoff the balance on a loan in the event of their default. In deeds of trust or mortgages where a power of sale exists, the power to
sell the property is given to the lender or their representative, typically referred to as the trustee. It requires that the debtor receive a notice of foreclosure only 25 days prior to the auction date.

Notice of Sale
A notice of sale must be recorded in the county where the property is located and then:
 (1) mailed to the borrower at least twenty-five (25) days before the sale

(2) published once a week for three (3) weeks, with the first publication appearing not less than twenty (20) days before the sale, in a newspaper of general circulation in the county where the property is located. The notice shall contain the time, date and place of sale, a description of the property and the default, as well as a "warning" to the borrower, informing him the property is going to be sold and what rights he has to stop the procedure. The trustee must also post similar notices in
three public places.

Right of Redemption
Borrowers have no rights of redemption.
*Courtesy of New Hampshire State Statutes

New Jersey*
New Jersey is a Judicial State
New Jersey Fair Foreclosure Act Letters:
Mortgage lenders must send the statutorily required notice letters prior to foreclosure referral. A title search must be ordered and received prior to filing a complaint. A title search is generally received within ten to twenty working days of our receipt of the file.

Complaint Filed:
Sheriff has 40 days in which to attempt to serve complaint on all defendants including all lien holders of record.
Complaint Served:
If service is unsuccessful, service may be made by alternative means after due and diligent inquiry. Service is the most difficult and time-consuming aspect of New Jersey mortgage foreclosure practice. Once served, defendants have 35 days to file an answer to the complaint.
If the USA or the State of New Jersey are defendants, those parties have 60 days to answer the complaint.

10/45 Day Default:
After service is completed on all defendants on default has been entered against them, the Fair Foreclosure Act requires Notice of Intent to Enter Foreclosure Judgment be sent to defendant/mortgagor, providing at final opportunity to cure the default. If defendant/mortgagor does not respond to the letter, the plaintiff must wait 45 days before entering judgment.

Judgment Entered/Writ Of Execution Issued/Sheriff's Sale Scheduled:

If no response to Complaint is filed by defendants, judgment may be entered for mortgage foreclosure and sale of the property. Simultaneously, a Writ of Execution is issued and is sent to the Sheriff to schedule a Sale. The Sheriff is required to schedule a Sale within 6 months of receipt of the Writ.

Sale Date:

Sales may be postponed twice by the lender and twice by the defendants. Any other postponements require a Court Order. Bidding instructions are required for all loans. Payment of all settlement charges must be made to the Sheriff within thirty days of the Sale or it may be declared null and void. Title and eviction information must be provided immediately after the Sale in order to calculate settlement charges and to provide the Sheriff with the appropriate Assignment of Bid.

Ejectment Procedures For New Jersey Judgment Entered and Writ of Possession Issued:

At the conclusion of the Sheriff's Sale, judgment may be entered for possession.
Simultaneously, a Writ of Possession is issued and the Sheriff has thirty days to serve the Writ of Possession on defendant.

Ejectment Date: After the Sheriff serves the Writ of Possession, the occupants are given twenty days to

move. On the twenty-first day after service of the Writ of Possession, if the occupants have not vacated the premises, the attorney telephones the Sheriff's Office to schedule the eviction. The Sheriff will then assign a date for the eviction,
which is usually 30 to 90 days from the date the judgment is entered. The client must provide for a moving company and locksmith at the time set by the Sheriff for the lockout.

Landlord/Tenant Act: If the property is occupied by a tenant, a separate complaint must be filed in Landlord/Tenant Court. This process may take 60-180 days.
*Courtesy of National Foreclosure Professionals and New Jersey State Statutes

New Mexico*
New Mexico is a Judicial State
Judicial-
A summons is submitted, a response is required within 25-30 days, if uncontested there will be entry of judgment, and the sheriff will publish and post notice of sale.

Notice of Sale
The notice of sale must contain a legal description of the property, the place, the time and the date of sale, which must be at least thirty (30) days after the notice of sale is issued, on which the foreclosure sale is to be held. The property will then be sold to the highest bidder on the

date specified in the notice.

The whole process takes a minimum of eight months to complete. Two months to default parties, four to six months until entry of judgment, and two more months before the sheriff publishes and posts the property for sale.

Redemption Period

In most cases, the borrower has up to nine (9) months to redeem the property by paying the amount of the highest bid at the foreclosure sale, plus fees, penalties and interest.

*Courtesv of New Mexico State Statutes
New York*
New York is a Judicial State
Judicial
Lawsuit is filed

The lender files a lawsuit. Like most judicial states, the lender begins by having a summons and a complaint is filed. It is then sent to the borrower asking them to come to court to answer the complaint. The complaint is a lawsuit, which describes the lenders basis for foreclosure action.

A notice of lis pendens is filed. The borrower has 20 days to answer the complaint. If no action is taken within the 20 days, there will be a motion for summary judgment. After summary judgment is granted, the court usually appoints a referee who will determine the amount owed and recommend how the property should be sold. Once the referee has issued the report, the court confirms the report and a judgment directing the sale of the property will be entered.

Notice of Sale
The foreclosure sale is advertised in a county newspaper for (4) four weeks. The sale is made by public auction to the highest bidder. The lender has the option of bidding. The lender must distribute the proceeds according to the terms of the judgment signed by the judge.

Deficiency Judgment
If proceeds from the sale do not produce sufficient funds, the lender has the right to issue a deficiency judgment against the borrower. The motion for a deficiency judgment must be within 90 days after the foreclosure auction or the lender loses this right.

Redemption Rights
There is no redemption period for the borrower
*Courtesy of New York State Statutes

North Carolina*
North Carolina is a Non-Judicial State
Right to Foreclose or Sell under Power.
All sales of real property, under a power of sale contained in any mortgage or deed of trust to secure the payment of money, by any mortgagee or trustee, through an agent or attorney for that purpose, appointed orally or in writing by such mortgagee or trustee, whether such writing has
been or shall be registered or not, shall be valid, whether or not such mortgagee or trustee was or shall be present at such sale.

179

Place of sale of real property.
(a)Every sale of real property shall be held in the county where the property is situated unless the property consists of a single tract situated in two or more counties.

(b) A sale of a single tract of real property situated in two or more counties may be held in anyone of the counties in which any part of the tract is situated. As used in this section, a "single tract" means any tract which has a continuous boundary, regardless of whether parts thereof
may have been acquired at different times or from different persons, or whether it may have been subdivided into other units or lots, or whether it is sold as a whole or in parts.

(c) When a mortgage or deed of trust with power of sale of real property designates the place of sale within the county, the sale shall be held at the place so designated.

(d) When a mortgage or deed of trust with power of sale of real property confers upon the mortgagee or trustee the right to designate the place of sale, the sale shall be held at the place designated by the notice of sale, which place shall be either on the premises to be sold or as follows:

(1) Property situated wholly within a single county shall be sold at the courthouse door of the county in which the land is situated.

(2) A single tract of property situated in two or more

counties may be sold at the courthouse door of anyone of the counties in which some part of the real property is situated.

(e) When a mortgage or deed of trust with power of sale of real property does not designate, or confer upon the mortgagee or trustee the right to designate, the place of sale, or when it designates as the place of sale some county in which no part of the property is situated, such real property shall be sold as follows:
(1) Property situated wholly within a single count shall be sold at the courthouse door of the county in which the land is situated.

(2) A single tract of property situated in two or more counties may be sold at the courthouse door of anyone of the counties in which some part of the real property is situated.

Requirement of cash deposit at sale.
(a)If a mortgage or deed of trust contains provisions with respect to a cash deposit at the sale, the terms of the instrument shall be complied with.
(b) If the instrument contains no provision with respect to a cash deposit at the sale, the mortgagee or trustee may require the highest bidder immediately to make a cash deposit not to exceed the greater of five percent (5%) of the amount of the bid or seven hundred fifty dollars ($750.00).
(c) If the highest bidder fails to make the required deposit, the person holding the sale may at the same time and place immediately re-offer the property for sale.

Notice of Sale and hearing.

The mortgagee or trustee granted a power of sale under a mortgage or deed of trust who seeks to exercise such power of sale shall file with the clerk of court a notice of hearing in accordance with the terms of this section. After the notice of hearing is filed, the notice of hearing shall be served upon each party entitled to notice under this section. The notice shall specify a time and place for the hearing before the clerk of court and shall be served not less than 10 days prior to
the date of such hearing. The notice shall be served and proof of service shall be made in any manner provided by the Rules of Civil Procedure for service of summons, including service by registered mail or certified mail, return receipt requested. However, in those instances that
publication would be authorized, posting a notice in a conspicuous may make service place and manner upon the property not less than 20 days prior to the date of the hearing, and if service upon a party cannot be effected after a reasonable and diligent effort in a manner authorized above, notice to such party may be given by posting the notice in a conspicuous place and manner upon the property not less than 20 days prior to the date of hearing. Service
by posting may run concurrently with any other effort to effect service. The notice shall be posted by the sheriff. In the event that the service is obtained by posting, an affidavit shall be filed with the clerk of court showing the circumstances warranting the use of service by posting.

If any party is not served or is not timely served prior to the date of the hearing, the clerk shall order the hearing continued to a date and time certain, not less than 10 days from the date scheduled for the original hearing. All notices already timely served remain effective. The mortgagee or trustee shall satisfy the notice requirement of this section with respect to those parties not served or not timely served with respect to the original hearing. Any party timely served, who has not received actual notice of the date to which the hearing has been continued, shall be sent the order of continuance by first-class mail at his last known address.

I\Jot ice of hearing shall be served in a manner authorized in subsection (a) upon:
1. Any person to whom the security interest instrument itself directs notice to be sent in case of default.

2. Any person obligated to repay the indebtedness against whom the holder thereof intends to assert liability therefore, and any such person not notified shall not be liable for any deficiency remaining after the sale.

3. Every record owner of the real estate whose interest is of record in the county where the real property is located at the time the notice of hearing is filed in that county. The term "record owner" means any person owning a present or future interest in the real property, which interest is of record at the time that the notice of hearing is filed and would be

affected by the foreclosure proceeding, but does not mean or include the trustee in a deed of trust or the owner or holder of
a mortgage, deed of trust, judgment, mechanic's or material man's lien, or other lien or security interest in the real property. Tenants in possession under unrecorded leases or rental agreements shall not be considered record owners.
I\Jot ice shall be in writing and shall state in a manner reasonably calculated to make the party entitled to notice aware of the following:

1. The particular real estate security interest being foreclosed, with such a description as is necessary to identify the real property, including the date, original amount, original holder, and book and page of the security instrument.
2. The name and address of the holder of the security instrument at the time that the notice of hearing is filed.
 3. The nature of the default claimed.
4. The fact, if such be the case, that the secured creditor has accelerated the maturity of the debt.
5. Any right of the debtor to pay the indebtedness or cure the default if such is permitted. The holder has confirmed in writing to the person giving the notice, or if the holder is giving the notice, the holder shall confirm in the notice, that, within 30 days of the date of the notice, the debtor was sent by first-class mail at the debtor's last known address a written statement of the amount of principal and interest that the holder claims in good faith is owed as of the date of the written statement, a daily interest charge based on

the contract rate as of the date of the statement, and the amount of other expenses the holder contends it is owed as of the date of the statement.

6. The right of the debtor (or other party served) to appear before the clerk of court at a time and on a date specified, at which appearance he shall be afforded the opportunity to show cause as to why the foreclosure should not be allowed to be held. The notice shall contain a statement that if the debtor does not intend to contest the creditor's allegations of default, the debtor does not have to appear at the hearing and that his failure to attend the hearing will not affect his right to pay the indebtedness and thereby prevent the proposed sale, or to attend the actual sale, should he elect to do so.

7. That if the foreclosure sale is consummated, the purchaser will be entitled to possession of the real estate as of the date of delivery of his deed, and that the debtor, if still in possession, can then be evicted. The name, address, and telephone number of the trustee or mortgagee.

8. That the debtor should keep the trustee or mortgagee notified in writing of his address so that he can be mailed copies of the notice of foreclosure setting forth the terms under which the sale will be held, and notice of any postponements or resale's.

Contents of notice of sale.

The notice of sale shall

1. Describe the instrument pursuant to which the sale is held, by identifying the original mortgagors and recording data. If the record owner is different from the original mortgagors,

the notice shall also list the record owner of the property, as reflected on the records of the register of deeds not more than 10 days prior to posting the notice. The notice may also
reflect the owner not reflected on the records if known;

2. Designate the date, hour and place of sale consistent with the provisions of the instrument and this Article;

3. Describe the real property to be sold in such a manner as is reasonably calculated to inform the public as to what is being sold, which description may be in general terms and may incorporate the description as used in the instrument containing the power of sale by reference thereto. Any property described in the instrument containing the power of sale, which is not being offered for sale should also be described in such a manner as to enable prospective purchasers to determine what is and what is not being offered for sale;

4. State the terms of the sale provided for by the instrument pursuant to which the sale is held, including the amount of the cash deposit, if any, to be made by the highest bidder at the sale;

5. State that the property will be sold subject to taxes and special assessments if it is to be so sold.

6. State whether the property is being sold subject to or together with any subordinate rights or interests provided those rights and interests are sufficiently identified

Posting and publishing notice of sale of real property.

In addition to complying with such provisions with respect to posting or publishing
notice of sale as are contained in the security instrument,
Notice of sale of real property shall
 1. Be posted, in the area designated by the clerk of superior court for posting public notices in
the county in which the property is situated, at least 20 days immediately preceding the sale.
2. The notice shall be published once a week for at least two successive weeks in a newspaper published and qualified for legal advertising in the county in which the property is situated.
3. If no such newspaper is published in the county, then notice shall be published once a week for at least two successive weeks in a newspaper having a general circulation in the county.
4. In addition to the required newspaper advertisement, the clerk may in his discretion, on application of any interested party, authorize such additional advertisement as in the opinion of the clerk will serve the interest of the parties, and permit the charges for such further advertisement to be taxed as a part of the costs of the foreclosure.
When the notice of sale is published in a newspaper
 1. The period from the date of the first publication to the date of the last publication, both dates inclusive, shall not be less than seven days, including Sundays, and
2. The date of the last publication shall be not more than 10 days preceding the date of the sale.
3. The notice of sale shall be mailed by first-class mail at least 20 days prior to the date of sale to each party

entitled to notice of the hearing whose address is known to the trustee or mortgagee and in addition shall also be mailed by first-class mail to any party desiring a copy of the notice of sale.

Time of sale.
A sale shall begin at the time designated in the notice of sale or as soon thereafter as practicable, but not later than one hour after the time fixed therefore unless it is delayed by
other sales held at the same place. The sale shall be held between the hours of 10:00 A.M. and 4:00 P.M. on any day other than Sunday or a legal holiday.

*Courtesy of North Carolina State Statutes

North Dakota*
North Dakota is a Judicial State
Action to foreclose mortgage on real estate authorized.
An action may be brought in the district court for the foreclosure or satisfaction of a mortgage
upon real property in accordance with the provisions of this chapter.
What complaint shall state.
In an action for the foreclosure or satisfaction of a mortgage, the complaint shall state whether any proceedings have been had at law or otherwise for the recovery of the debt secured by such mortgage, or any part thereof, and if there have been, whether any and what part thereof has been collected. The plaintiff shall also state in the complaint whether the

plaintiff will in a later and separate action demand judgment for any deficiency, which may remain due to the plaintiff after sale of the mortgaged premises against every party who is personally liable for the debt secured
by the mortgage.

Summons -How served.
In addition to any other method provided by law for the service of summons, in all actions for the foreclosure or satisfaction of a mortgage, or other lien, upon real estate, in any court of this state, the summons may be served personally upon all defendants, if any, in actual possession
of the real estate involved in the action, if such real estate is occupied, and upon all other defendants by publication in the manner provided in this chapter. When the summons is thus
served the service shall be deemed complete.

Notice before foreclosure.
At least thirty days and not more than ninety days before the commencement of any action or proceeding for the foreclosure of a mortgage on real estate, a written notice shall be served on the title owner of record of the real estate described in the mortgage as shown by the records in
the office of the recorder of the county in which such real estate is situated.

Contents of notice.
The notice before foreclosure shall contain:
1. A description of the real estate.

2. The date and amount of the mortgage.

3. The amount due for principal, interest, and taxes paid by the owner of the mortgage, stated separately.

4. A statement that if the amount due is not paid within thirty days from the date of the mailing or service of the notice proceedings will be commenced to foreclose the mortgage.

Notice may be served by registered or certified mail.
The notice before foreclosure may be served by registered or certified mail addressed to the owner of record at the owner's post-office address as such address is shown by the mortgage or by the records in the chain of title to such real estate in the office of the recorder of the county where the real estate is situated. If such post-office address is not shown in the mortgage or in such records, the notice may be served by registered or certified mail addressed to the owner of record at the post office nearest any part or tract of the real estate.

Certificate of sale -Deed and effect.
Whenever any real property shall be sold under judgment of foreclosure pursuant to the provisions of this chapter, the officer or other person making the sale must give to the purchaser a certificate of sale and at the expiration of the time for the redemption of such property, if the same is not redeemed, the person or officer making the sale, or the successor in

office, or other officer appointed by the court, must make to the purchaser, the purchaser's heirs, or assigns, or to any person who has acquired the title of such purchaser by redemption or otherwise, a deed or deeds of such property. Such deed shall vest in the grantee all the right, title, and interest of the mortgagor in and to the property sold, at the time the mortgage was executed, or subsequently acquired by the mortgagor, and shall be a bar to all claim, right, or equity of redemption in or to
the property by the parties to such action, their heirs and personal representatives, and also against all persons claiming under them, or any of them, subsequent to the commencement of the action in which such judgment was rendered.

Application of proceeds.
The proceeds of every foreclosure sale must be applied to the discharge of the debt adjudged by the court to be due and of the costs, and if there is any surplus, it must be brought into court for the use of the defendant or of the person entitled thereto, subject to the order of the court.

When there is a surplus.
If the surplus upon a foreclosure sale, or any part thereof, shall remain in court for the term of three months without being applied for, the judge of the district court may direct the same to be put out at interest for benefit of the defendant, the defendant's representatives, or assigns,
subject to the order of the court.

Complaint dismissed on payment of installments due.
Whenever an action shall be commenced for the foreclosure of a mortgage upon which there shall be due any interest, or any portion or installment of the principal, and there shall be other portions or installments to become due subsequently, the complaint shall be dismissed upon the defendant's bringing into court at any time before decree of sale the principal and interest due, with costs and disbursements.

Redemption Period.
All real property sold upon foreclosure of a mortgage by order, judgment, or decree of court may be redeemed at any time within one year after such sale.

*Courtesy of North Dakota State Statutes

Ohio*
Ohio is a judicial state.

Foreclosure actions are commenced with the filing of a complaint, naming as Defendants all parties having ownership interest, lien or other encumbrance on the property. Service of the summons is perfected generally by mail, or by publication if a party cannot be located. Unless
the mortgagor files an answer to the complaint within 28 days after service of the summons, a motion for default judgment can be filed. Otherwise, the case will proceed based upon a motion for summary judgment or trial. A foreclosure decree setting forth the rights of

the various parties is submitted for approval by the court. Once the foreclosure decree is approved and filed, an order of sale is issued to the Sheriff, who then retains, 3 fee holders to act as appraisers.

The Sheriff will schedule the Sheriff's Sale for an auction, and publish a notice of the Sale for at least 30 days prior to the Sale date in a newspaper of general circulation in the county in which the property is located. The minimum bid at the Sheriff's Sale is 2/3 of the Sheriff's appraisal proceedings. The sheriff will conduct the sale at the courthouse and the property will be sold to the highest bidder. Unless there is an irregularity, the court files an order confirming the Sheriff's sale. The mortgagor has a statutory right to redeem the property by paying the balance due
together with the court costs, only until the filing of the order confirming the Sale. Uncontested foreclosures generally take 6-10 months. Evictions can be accomplished through a writ of possession through the Sheriff, in the event the
occupants were named as parties in the foreclosure action and served with a summons.

Otherwise, possession may only be recovered through a municipal court eviction action. In either cases, the process takes approximately 6 weeks until the move out.
Deficiency judgments are fully enforceable, but there is a 2-year statute of limitations to collect in the event judgment was rendered prior to confirmation the Sheriff's sale and the property was a dwelling with 2

units or less.

Oklahoma*
Oklahoma is primarily a Judicial State.
The process of foreclosure begins by filing a lawsuit. This allows for the court to order the foreclosure. There is a filing of lis pendens. The court issues judgment and affidavit of judgment is filed with county clerk. After court declares foreclosure, there is a special order of sale. The property must be appraised before it goes to auction.

Notice of Sale
The notice of sale must be published in a newspaper in the county where the property is located once a week for at least (3) consecutive weeks, with the first publishing being not less than thirty (25) days before the sale. Mailings will be sent out to current owners of the property notifying them of the sale.

Sheriffs Sale
The property must be sold at public auction to the highest bidder at the time and on the date specified in the notice. The highest bidder at the must post cash or certified funds equal to ten (10) percent of the bid amount. If the highest bidder is unable to do so, then the lender may proceed with the sale and accept the next highest bid. The property may not be sold for less than two-thirds of the appraised value. The

lender may issue a deficiency judgment, as long as it is
with in 90 days of the foreclosure sale.

Redemption Period
There is no redemption period in Oklahoma
*Courtesy of Oklahoma State Statutes

Oregon*
Oregon is a judicial and non-judicial state.
* The majority of loans are foreclosed by the non-judicial method.

Default Date Sale

Major Elements of Oregon Foreclosures include:
1 Sending the Notice of Default out for recording and setting a sale date. (Must record Notice of Default, mail and serve Notice of Sale on occupants more than 120 days before the sale date).
2 Publication -4 consecutive weeks, the last publication must be more than 20 days before the sale date.
3 Sale date is set no earlier than 120 days from the Notice of Default.
4 The sale must be conducted between 9 a.m. and 4 p.m. at a place designated in the notice
5 Occupant of premises has 10 days after sale to vacate premises.
6 Sale can be continued up to 180 days (in case of Bankruptcy filing, sale continued indefinitely).

7 A deficiency judgment cannot be obtained through a non-judicial deed of trust foreclosure by advertisement.

*Courtesy of National Foreclosure Professionals and Oregon State Statutes

Pennsylvania**
Pennsylvania is a Judicial State
PA-Act 6 and PA. Act 91 Demand/Housing Assistance Notice Letters:

Mortgage lenders must send the statutorily required notice letters prior to foreclosure referral.
A title search must be ordered and received prior to filing a complaint. A title search is generally received within ten to twenty working days of our receipt of the file.

Complaint Filed:
Sheriff has 30 days in which to serve Complaint or it expires and must be reinstated (usually served, on the average, within twenty days after Complaint is filed).

Complaint Served:
Defendants have twenty days to file a response (either preliminary objections or answer or both) to the Complaint. If no response, then Plaintiff must forward ten-day Notice to Defendants. This Notice advises Defendants that if they do not take action within ten days of the Notice, Judgment
will be entered against them. If the USA is a Defendant, Judgment must be delayed for 90 days.

Judgment Entered/Writ of Executive Issued/Sheriff's Sale Scheduled:

If no response to Complaint is filed by Defendants and ten-day Notice expires, judgment may be entered for mortgage foreclosure and sale of the property. Simultaneously, a Writ of Execution is issued and the Sheriff's Sale is scheduled. The Defendants must be served the Notice of Sheriffs Sale at least 30 days prior to the Sheriff's Sale date. In addition, all lien holders must be served, by mail 30 days prior to a sale. The individual Sheriff's departments set a monthly Sale schedule.

There is generally a two-month to four-month period of time from the filing of the Writ until the actual Sale date.

Sale Date:

Sales may be postponed once and rescheduled within the next 10-day period. Any other postponements require a Court order. Bidding instructions are required for all loans. Payment of all settlement charges must be made to the Sheriff within thirty days of the Sale or it may be declared null and void. Title and eviction information must be provided immediately after the Sale in order to calculate settlement charges.

Ejectment Procedures
Complaint Filed:

Sheriff has 30 days in which to serve Complaint or it expires and must be reinstated (usually served on the average within twenty days after Complaint is filed).

Complaint Served:
Defendants have twenty days to file response to the Complaint. If no response, then Plaintiff must forward ten-day Notice to Defendants.

Judgment Entered And Write Of Possession Issued:
If no response to Complaint is filed by Defendants and ten-day Notice expires, judgment may be entered for Possession. Simultaneously, a Writ of Possession is issued and the Sheriff has thirty days to serve the Writ of Possession on Defendant.

Ejectment Date:
After the Sheriff serves the Writ of Possession, the occupants are given twenty days to move. On the twenty-first day after service of the Writ of Possession, if the occupants have not vacated the premises, the attorney telephones the Sheriff's office to schedule the eviction. The Sheriff will then assign a date for the eviction, which is usually 30 to 90 days from the date the judgment is entered. The client must provide for a moving company and locksmith at the time set by the Sheriff for the lockout.

Pennsylvania Act 6 And Act 91 Requirements

Loan Type Notice of Intention to Homeowner's Emergency
Mortgage Assistance Notice (PA Act 91)
Foreclose (PA Act 6)
Type of Mail Certified or Registered Mail Regular

Mail with Certificate of Mailing
Send To Property Address and Last Known Mailing Address Property Address and Last Known Mailing Address
Addressed To Each Record Owner(s) and Each Record Owner(s) Each Original Mortgagors
FHA Under
$50,000 Act 6 Required Act 91 Not Required
FHA Over
$50,000 Act 6 Not Required * Act 91 Not Required
VA/Conventional
Loans Under
$50,000
Act 6 Required Act 91 Required
VA/Conventional
Loans Over
$50,000
Act 6 Not Required* Act 91 Required
* A Demand Letter is generally required prior to commencing any foreclosure action. Please consult the specific mortgage for details on the type and content of the Preforeclosure notice to be sent.

**Courtesy of National Foreclosure Professionals and Pennsylvania State Statutes

Rhode Island*
Rhode Island is a non-judicial State Time Line/Non-Judicial (Statutory) Foreclosures

Complaint to foreclose.
Any person entitled to foreclose the equity of

redemption in any mortgaged estate, whether real or personal, may prefer a complaint to foreclose it, which complaint may be heard, tried, and determined according to the usages in chancery and the principles of equity.

Right of mortgagee to bid at sale.
At any sale by public auction made under and according to the provisions of any mortgage of real estate, or of any power of sale contained therein or annexed thereto, the mortgagee in the deed of mortgage or other conveyance, or pledge, his, her, or their assigns, or his, her, or their
heirs, executors or administrators, or any person for him, her, or them, may fairly and in good faith bid for and purchase the estate or property so put up for sale, or any part thereof, in the same manner as it may be bid for and purchased by any other person.

Discharge of purchaser at sale by payments to mortgagee.
The receipt in writing of a mortgagee shall be a sufficient discharge for any money accruing from sales made under the powers of sale conferred by his or her mortgage; and a person paying it to the mortgagee shall not be obliged to inquire whether any money remains due under the
mortgage, or to see as to the application of such proceeds in case of sale.
Publication of notice under power of sale.

Whenever any real estate shall be sold under any power of sale mortgage executed subsequent to May

4, 1911, and the mortgage shall provide for the giving of notice of the sale
by publication in some public newspaper at least once a week for three (3) successive weeks before the sale, the first publication of the notice shall be at least twenty-one (21) days before the day of sale, including the day of the first publication in the computation. Provided, however, that no notice shall be valid or effective unless the mortgagor has been mailed written notice of the time and place of sale by certified mail return receipt requested at the address of the real estate and, if different, at the mortgagor's address listed with the tax assessor's office of the city or town where the real estate is located or any other address mortgagor designates by written notice to mortgagee at his, her, or its last known address, at least twenty (20) days for mortgagors other than individual consumer mortgagors, and at least thirty (30) days for individual consumer mortgagors, days prior to the first publication, including the day of mailing in the computation. The mortgagee shall include in the foreclosure deed an
affidavit of compliance with this provision.

Mortgage foreclosure advertisement.
An advertisement for foreclosure may, if describing the real estate being foreclosed, describe the real estate to be foreclosed by metes and bounds description and street address, or by recitation of the taxing authority's assessor's plat and lot designation and street address, or by recitation of the book and page of mortgage and street address.

The Sale

The sale must be made by the sheriff of such county, or his deputy, between the hours of 9:00 am and 5:00 pm to the highest bidder. Any person including the mortgagee (lender) may bid at the sale. The winning bidder will receive a certificate of sale.

Deficiency Judgments

Obtaining deficiency judgments and actions for possession require "judicial steps" and are performed separately from the foreclosure sale.

*Courtesy of National Foreclosure Professionals and Rhode Island State Statutes

South Carolina*
South Carolina is a judicial state. Judicial Sales -No Deficiency Demanded

Debt secured must be established before sale by mortgagee.
No sale under or by virtue of any mortgage or other instrument in writing intended as security for a debt, conferring a power upon the mortgagee or creditor to sell the mortgaged or pledged property while such power remains of force or has not been revoked by the death of the person executing such mortgage or instrument, shall be valid to pass the title of the land mortgaged unless the debt for which the security is given shall be first established by the

judgment of some court of competent jurisdiction or unless the amount of the debt be consented to in writing by the
debtor subsequently to the maturity of the debt, such consent in writing to be recorded in the office of the register of deeds or clerk of the court where the mortgage or other instrument in writing given to secure such debt is or ought to be recorded. But if the mortgagor be dead it shall not be necessary in any foreclosure proceeding first to establish the debt by the judgment of some court of competent jurisdiction in order to obtain a decree of foreclosure and sale.

Court may render judgment and order sale at same time.

The court may also render judgment against the parties liable for the payment of the debt secured by the mortgage and direct at the same time the sale of the mortgaged premises. Such judgment so rendered may be entered and docketed in the clerk's office in the same manner as other judgments. Upon the sale of the mortgaged premises the officer making the sale under the order of the court shall credit upon the judgment so rendered for the debt the amount paid to the plaintiff from the proceeds of the sale.

Application for order of appraisal.

(A) In any real estate foreclosure proceeding a defendant against whom a personal judgment is taken or asked, whether he has theretofore appeared in the action or not, may within thirty days after the sale of the mortgaged property apply by verified petition to the clerk of court in which the decree or order of sale was taken for an order of appraisal.

(B) Except in any real estate foreclosure proceeding relating to a dwelling place or to a consumer credit transaction, a defendant against whom a personal judgment may be taken on a real estate secured transaction may waive the appraisal rights as provided by this section if the debtors, makers, borrowers, and/or guarantors are notified in writing before the transaction that a waiver of appraisal rights will be required and upon signing a statement during the transaction similar to the following:
"The laws of South Carolina provide that in any real estate foreclosure preceding a defendant against whom a personal judgment is taken or asked may within thirty days after the sale of the mortgaged property apply to the court for an order of appraisal. The statutory appraisal value as approved by the court would be substituted for the high bid and may decrease the amount of any deficiency owing in connection with the transaction. THE UNDERSIGNED HEREBY WAIVES AND RELINQUISHES THE STATUTORY APPRAISAL RIGHTS WHICH MEANS THE HIGH BID AT THE JUDICIAL FORECLOSURE SALE WILL BE APPLIED TO THE DEBT REGARDLESS OF ANY APPRAISED VALUE OF THE MORTGAGED PROPERTY."

Notice of Sale
A notice of sale will usually contain a description of the property, the time and place of sale, the borrowers name, the lenders name and must be published at the

courthouse door and two other public places at least three weeks before the sale. The notice must also be published in a local newspaper of general circulation where the property resides for at least 3 consecutive weeks.
The sale will be held on the first Monday in each month, unless it is a holiday, If the sale lands on a holiday, then the sale may take place on the following Tuesday. The sale may begin at 11:00 am and go until 5:00 pm, but the sheriff may close the bidding prior to that time.

Deficiency judgment/ Redemption Period.
In actions to foreclose mortgages the court may adjudge and direct the payment by the mortgagor of any residue of the mortgage debt that may remain unsatisfied after a sale of the
mortgaged premises in cases in which the mortgagor shall be personally liable for the debt secured by such mortgage and if the mortgage debt be secured by the covenant or obligation of any person other than the mortgagor the plaintiff may make such person a party to the action and
the court may adjudge payment of the residue of such debt remaining unsatisfied after a sale of the mortgaged premises against such other person and may enforce such judgment as in other cases.

Borrowers have no rights to redeem the property after it goes to auction.
*Courtesy of National Foreclosure Professionals and South Carolina State Statutes

South Dakota*
South Dakota is a judicial State
A complaint initiating a civil action is to be served. All parties are given 30 days to answer. Once judgment is entered, there is a 30 day stay that can be waived by the court.

Notice of Sale
Following the period, notice of sale must be given by publication once a week for four successive weeks in a newspaper where the property is located. At least 21 days before the sale of the property, the lender must serve a written copy of the notice of foreclosure sale to the borrower
and any lien holder whose interest in the property being foreclosed would be affected by the foreclosure. Once publication is complete, the sale is conducted.

The sale will be conducted between the hours of 9:00 am and 5:00 pm. Any person including the mortgagee (lender) may bid at the sale. The winning bidder will receive a certificate of sale.

Redemption Period
In most cases, borrowers have 1 year from the date of sale to redeem the property.
*Courtesy of South Dakota State Statutes

Tennessee*
Tennessee is a Non-Judicial State
Foreclosure Sale

Where, upon the foreclosure of a mortgage or deed of trust, or in any case, the specified land to be sold is mentioned in the decree, the court, upon the application of the complainant, may order that:

(l)The property be sold on a credit of not less than six (6) months nor more than two (2) years.
 (2) When the sale is made, and reported and confirmed, no right of redemption or repurchase shall exist in the debtor or the debtor's creditors, but that the purchaser's title shall be absolute.

(3) The surplus of the purchase money, or the bonds or notes taken therefore, over and above what is necessary to pay the complainant's debt, be paid to the debtor or the debtor's other creditors entitled to the same.

Twenty days' notice by publication
 (a) In any sale of land to foreclose a deed of trust, mortgage or other lien securing the payment of money or other thing of value or under judicial orders or process, advertisement of such sale shall be made at least three (3) different times in some newspaper published in the county where the sale is to be made.

(b) The first publication shall be at least twenty (20) days previous to the sale.

(c) The provisions of this section shall not apply where the amount of indebtedness for the payment of which the property being sold does not amount to

more than two hundred dollars ($200), in which event the owner of the property may order that advertisement be made by
written notices posted, instead of by notices published in a newspaper.

(d) Nothing in this section shall be construed as applying to any notice published in accordance with any contract entered into heretofore, and expressed in a mortgage, deed of trust or other legal instruments.

(e) If no newspaper is published in the county in which the land is to be sold, the advertisement in a newspaper is dispensed with, unless ordered by court.

Posting written notices

Whenever the advertisement cannot be made in a newspaper, the officer shall make publication of the sale for thirty (30) days by written notices posted in at least five
(5) of the most public places in the county, one (1) of which shall be the courthouse door, and another in the neighborhood of the defendant; if of realty, in the civil district where the land lies.

Contents of advertisement or notice

The advertisement or notice shall:

(1) Give the names of the plaintiff and defendant, or parties interested
 (2) Describe the land in brief terms, including the

street address if available
 (3) Mention the time and place of sale

Time of sale
The sale in all these cases shall be made between the hours of ten o'clock a.m. (10:00 a.m.) and four o'clock p.m. (4:00 p.m.) of the day fixed in the notice or advertisement.
*Courtesy of Tennessee State Statutes

Texas*
Texas is a Non-Judicial State
The lender gives the debtor in default a written notice or demand letter. The borrower is given 20 days to cure the loan before the debt is declared due and notice of sale is given. The lender will then instruct the trustee to proceed with the foreclosure process.
A sale of real property under a power of sale conferred by a deed of trust or other contract lien must be a public sale at auction held between 10 a.m. and 4 p.m. of the first Tuesday of a month.
The sale must take place at the county courthouse in the county in which the land is located, or if the property is located in more than one county, the sale may be made at the courthouse in any county in which the property is located. The commissioners court shall designate the area at the courthouse where the sales are to take place and shall record the designation in the real property records of the county. The sale must occur in the designated area. If no area is designated by the commissioners court, the notice of sale must designate the area at the courthouse where the sale covered by that notice is to take place,

and the sale must occur in that area.

 (b) Notice of the sale, which must include a statement of the earliest time at which the sale will begin, must be given at least 21 days before the date of the sale:

(1) by posting at the courthouse door of each county in which the property is located a written notice designating the county in which the property will be sold;

(2) by filing in the office of the county clerk of each county in which the property is located a copy of the notice posted under Subdivision (1); and

(3) by the holder of the debt to which the power of sale is related serving written notice of the sale by certified mail on each debtor who, according to the records of the holder of the debt, is obligated to pay the debt.

(c) The sale must begin at the time stated in the notice of sale or not later than three hours after that time.

(d) Notwithstanding any agreement to the contrary, the holder of the debt shall serve a debtor in default under a deed of trust or other contract lien on real property used as the debtor's residence with written notice by certified mail stating that the debtor is in default under the deed of trust or other contract lien and giving the debtor at least 20 days to cure the default before notice of sale can be

given under Subsection (b). The entire calendar day on which the notice required by this subsection is given, regardless of the time of day at which the notice is given, is included in computing the 20-day notice period required by this subsection, and the entire calendar day on which notice of sale is given under Subsection (b) is excluded in computing the 20-day notice
period.

(e) Service of a notice under this section by certified mail is complete when the notice is deposited in the United States mail, postage prepaid and addressed to the debtor at the debtor's last known address as shown by the records of the holder of the debt. The affidavit of a person knowledgeable of the facts to the effect that service was completed is prima facie evidence of service.

(f) Each county clerk shall keep all notices filed under Subdivision (2) of Subsection

(b) in a convenient file that is available to the public for examination during normal business hours. The clerk may dispose of the notices after the date of sale specified in the notice has passed. The clerk shall receive a fee of $2 for each notice filed.

(g) The entire calendar day on which the notice of sale is given, regardless of the time of day at which the notice is given, is included in computing the 21-day notice period required by Subsection (b), and the entire calendar day of the foreclosure sale is excluded.

Right of Redemption
There is no right of redemption in Texas.
*Courtesy of Texas State Statutes

Utah*
Utah is a non-judicial state
Utah's Trust Deed statutes, which model the California Act, have been in place since 1961. Because the private power of sale has been conferred on trustees of real estate Trust Deeds by Utah Code, Trust Deeds in Utah are foreclosed non-judicially. The entire process takes approximately four and one-half months, the detail of which is included in subsequent paragraphs.

The foreclosure work is commenced on a file once the referral package is received. This should include a current status sheet on the loan, copies of the Trust Deed Note, Trust Deed, all assignments, title policy and Mortgage Insurance Certificate (if available) and possibly the Substitution of Trustee. If your foreclosure referral package includes the Substitution of Trustee, the Notice of Default will be immediately prepared and both documents recorded within 10 days of the date the referral is received. Preparing the Substitution and sending it back for execution by overnight mail will add approximately two weeks to the time before recording the Notice of Default.

After recording the Substitution of Trustee and Notice of Default, copies of these papers must be mailed to the Trustors, as well as all others who have recorded a written
request for the receipt of any notices filed, within 10 days of the recording date. As a matter of practice, notices are mailed to all persons appearing to have an interest in the property as determined by the foreclosure title report.

Sale of trust property --Power of trustee -- Foreclosure of trust deed.
The trustee is given the power of sale by which the trustee may exercise and cause the trust property to be sold, after a breach of an obligation for which the trust property is conveyed as security; or, at the option of the beneficiary, a trust deed may be foreclosed in the manner provided by law for the foreclosure of mortgages on real property. The power of sale may be exercised by the trustee without express provision for it in the trust deed.

Sale of trust property by trustee --Notice of default.
The power of sale conferred upon the trustee may not be exercised until:
(1) the trustee first files for record, in the office of the recorder of each county where the trust property or some part or parcel of the trust property is situated, a notice of default, identifying the trust deed by stating the name of the trustor named in the trust deed and giving the book and
page, or the recorder's entry number, where the trust

deed is recorded and a legal description of the trust property, and containing a statement that a breach of an obligation for which the trust property was conveyed as security has occurred, and setting forth the nature of that breach and

of the trustee's election to sell or cause to be sold the property to satisfy the obligation;

(2) not less than three months has elapsed from the time the trustee filed for record under Subsection (1); and

(3) after the lapse of at least three months the trustee shall give notice of sale

Notice of trustee's sale --Description of property -- Time and place of sale.

The trustee shall give written notice of the time and place of sale particularly describing the property to be sold:

(a) by publication of the notice:

(i) at least three times;

(ii) once a week for three consecutive weeks;

(iii) the last publication to be at least ten days but not more than 30 days before the date the sale is scheduled; and

(iv) in a newspaper having a general circulation in each county in which the property to be sold, or some part of the property to be sold, is situated; and

(b) by posting the notice:

(i) at least 20 days before the date the sale is scheduled; and

(ii) (A) in some conspicuous place on the property to be sold; and

(6) at the office of the county recorder of each county in which the trust property, or some part of it, is located.

(2) (a) The sale shall be held at the time and place designated in the notice of sale.

(b) The time of sale shall be between the hours of 8 a.m. and 5 p.m.

(c) The place of sale shall be clearly identified in the notice of sale under Subsection (1) and shall be at a courthouse serving the county in which the property to be sold, or some part of the property to be sold, is located.

(d) High bidder must pay $5000 down and the remaining sale price within 24 hours.

(3) The notice of sale shall be in substantially the following form: Notice of Trustee's Sale

The following described property will be sold at public auction to the highest bidder, payable in lawful money of the United States at the time of sale, at (insert location of sale) on (month\day\year), at _.m. of said day, for the purpose of foreclosing a trust deed originally executed by __ (and __, his wife,) as trustors, in favor of__, covering real property located at , and more particularly described as:

(Insert legal description) The current beneficiary of the trust deed is and the record owners of the property as of the

recording of the notice of default are

Dated (month\day\year).

Trustee

The Trustors, fee title owner or any creditor has the right to reinstate the loan delinquency within three months after the date of recording by paying all delinquent installments, late charges, inspection fees and the foreclosure fees and costs. If not reinstated during this three month period, the matter is set for a Trustee's Sale which takes place four or five weeks after the end of the reinstatement period. It is optional with
the beneficiary whether a reinstatement will be accepted after the three month reinstatement period has ended. However, the V.A. regulations require the beneficiary to accept a reinstatement right up to the time of sale, and H.U.D. strongly recommends it.

After the sale takes place, a Trustee's Deed to the successful bidder will be prepared. This is usually H.U.D., V.A. or the beneficiary of the conventional loan. Trustee's Deeds on conventional loans will be prepared and sent for recording approximately one week following the sale. On V.A. loans, the Trustee's Deed is recorded in the name of the beneficiary and a Special Warranty Deed from the beneficiary to the V.A. is subsequently recorded. The V.A. requires that both deeds be recorded within seven days following the date of sale. Due to H.U.D. regulations that need to be met, the Trustee's Deeds on F.H.A. loans is prepared immediately, but awaits approval before being recorded.

At the time the Trustee's Deed is recorded, the necessary title work is ordered to show clear title to the purchaser. Experience has shown that it may take ten days to obtain the title packages.

As soon as the final title package is received, a copy is sent to the client's office, along with the foreclosure bill. The original title package is mailed to F.H.A. or the V.A. as appropriate. This completes the foreclosure process.

Occasionally this process is interrupted by bankruptcy, an eviction, or title problems. Mortgages are also valid in Utah, but are not often used. The foreclosure of a mortgage requires court action. Only one or two percent of Utah loans are secured by Mortgages rather than Trust Deeds. The process of foreclosing a Mortgage takes approximately eight and one-half months.

Utah Non-Judicial Trust Deed Foreclosure Timeline
Week 1
The file is opened the day it is received and reviewed. It is assigned a file number and entered into a computer system. If a Substitution of Trustee is received with the referral package, a Notice of Default is then prepared and recorded within ten days of receipt of the referral. If a Substitution is not included with the referral, one is prepared and sent to the client for execution by overnight mail delivery.
Week 2
As soon as the documents are recorded, a foreclosure title report is ordered. A conformed copy of the recorded Notice of Default and Substitution of Trustee are mailed to the original trustors, present

owners, and all other parties with a recorded interest by certified mail. The client is notified by letter of the recording date, when the three month reinstatement period will end, and the estimated sale date.

Week 15

At the end of the three month reinstatement period, the file will be pulled and set for a Trustee's Sale. The Trustee's Sale is held approximately five weeks after the reinstatement period ends.
The Notice of Trustee's Sale is mailed to the original trustors, present owners, and all other parties with a recorded interest by certified mail. The Notice of Trustee's Sale must be published in a newspaper having general circulation within the county the property is located, once a week
for three consecutive weeks, the last publication being at least 10 days prior but not more than 30 days prior to the sale. The Notice of Trustee's Sale must also be posted on the property and 3 other public places within the same county the property is located at least 20 days prior to the
sale. The client will be notified by letter of the sale date and will be asked for bidding instructions prior to the sale.

Week 20
The Trustee's Sale is held and a Trustee's Deed is prepared conveying the property to the highest bidder at the sale. If the property is purchased by HUD, the Trustee's Deed is held until notified to record it. A copy of the unrecorded deed is sent to the client for

their claim. If it is a conventional loan, the Trustee's Deed is recorded immediately, and a conformed copy is sent to the client. If it is a VA loan, the Trustee's Deed is recorded in the name of the beneficiary and a Special Warranty Deed from the beneficiary to the VA is subsequently recorded. The VA requires both deeds to be recorded within seven days following the date of sale. A conformed copy of each document is sent to our client as well as to the VA. After the Trustee's Deed is recorded, a final title package is ordered which upon receipt is forwarded to the client, HUD or the VA, whichever applies.
*Courtesy of National Foreclosure Professionals and Utah State Statutes

Vermont*
Vermont is a Judicial State
The entity bringing forth the action files the assignment and a notice is sent to the defendants to appear in court. One may file a motion with the complaint. The defendants must file an answer of the court will enter a default judgment. The plaintiff may also move for summary judgment. Judgment is made and the plaintiff prepares the foreclosure decree. The defendants have five days to object to the decree.

Notice of Sale
Notice of sale should be published at least thirty (30) days prior to auction, a notice of intent to foreclose must also be sent to the borrower by registered or certified mail at his or her last known address. The notice of intent must include information on the mortgage to be foreclosed, state the

current condition and the lenders right to accelerate the mortgage. It must also include the total amount necessary to cure the defaulted loan. The borrower must also be informed that he or she is entitled to receive a notice of sale at least sixty (60) days prior to the date of sale.

The borrower holds the right to redeem the property at any time prior to the foreclosure sale by paying the full amount due on the mortgage, plus any legal fees, and costs incurred during foreclosure.

The sale must be held on the property itself, unless otherwise ordered by the court. The property must be sold to the highest bidder. Anyone may bid at the sale, including the lender.

The borrower is entitled to receive any surplus from the sale.

Deficiency Judgment
Lenders hold the right to sue for deficiency if the sale price is not enough to cover the amount of the mortgage in default.

Redemption Period
Defendants will have a six month redemption period.
*Courtesy of Vermont State Statutes

Virginia*
Virginia is a non-judicial state.

Day 1

Review of file, acknowledgment of receipt of referral and preparation and forwarding of Substitution of Trustee to lender for execution. With Absolute Wireless the referral acknowledgment the client will be advised of any missing documentation. Virginia law requires that the Trustee receive a written request from the lender to proceed with foreclosure. The Trustee needs (1) the original note and copy of the deed of trust, (2) copy of default/breach letter and (3) the tide insurance policy. Note: If the original note has been lost a copy with a lost note affidavit will suffice, but the lender, prior to the institution of the foreclosure, must give the obligor(s), including the property owner, written notice that the original note is unavailable and that a request for sale by the Trustee will be made upon expiration of 14 days from the date of the notice. This notice must be sent certified mail, return receipt requested, to the last known address of the obligor(s) and must include the name and address of the Trustee and must further advise the obligor(s) that if he believes that he may be subject to a claim by a person other than the lender to enforce it he may petition the circuit court of the city or county wherein the property lies for an order requiring the lender to provide adequate protection against any such claim. The Trustee cannot proceed to sale without either the original note or the lost note notice (with the return receipt or returned envelope).

Days 2-14

Examination and review of title. The lender and title insurer are advised of any title defects and appropriate steps are undertaken to clear any title defects.

Days 15-20
Preparation of foreclosure notices to owners of record title and any others liable on the note. The minimum notice is 14 days prior to the date of the sale. Additionally, if there are IRS liens, homeowners' or condominium association liens or junior deed of trust, lien notice must be given to these lien holders as well. Simultaneously, with the foreclosure notice, the newspaper advertisement of sale is prepared and forwarded to the appropriate newspaper for publication.

The language of the deed of trust usually controls the advertising required. The minimum advertisement required in Virginia is, if weekly, once a week for 2 successive weeks, or if daily, once a day for 3 successive days. If the deed of trust is silent on the number of publications then it must be advertised once a week for 4 successive weeks. However, if the property lies within a city or in a county contiguous to a city, daily publication for 5 days, which may be consecutive, is deemed adequate.

Day 50
The foreclosure sale is held. The Trustee conducts the sale. Virginia law allows the lender to submit to the Trustee a written one-price bid in advance of the sale. The Trustee cannot bid actively on behalf of the

lender but can open the bidding at the one-price bid of the lender. A bidder's deposit of 10% of the successful bid is required at the time of sale. If the lender is the successful bidder this is waived. The lender is advised of the sale results immediately following the sale.

Days 51-65
Assuming the lender is the successful bidder, the proposed foreclosure deed, a copy of the proposed accounting, a "receipt" for the net sale proceeds and an invoice for the expenses of sale, including the cost of recording the foreclosure deed, is submitted to the lender. Upon
receipt of the requested funds and the "receipt" the deed is recorded and costs are paid. At this point, except for the accounting, the foreclosure is complete. Except for the IRS lien situations, there is no right of redemption in Virginia. If a third party is the successful bidder the Trustee coordinates the settlement with the bidder's attorney and proceeds to closing. If the successful bidder defaults, the bidder's deposit is used to pay the expenses of the foreclosure with the excess funds forwarded to the lender and the process begins again.

Days 90-100
The Trustee is required to file an accounting of the sale with the Commissioner of Accounts within 6 months of the date of the foreclosure sale. Included in this report is the accounting,
copies of the canceled checks for all sale expenses, the original note (or lost note affidavit and lost note

notice with receipts) and a copy of the recorded foreclosure deed.

Insurer Guarantor Requirements

FHA and VA regulations set forth specific time requirements for the institution and completion of the foreclosure process which must be met by the servicer in order to maintain the loan guaranty. The typical "time-line" previously set forth well exceeds these requirements. Daily monitoring of all pending foreclosures allows the firm to be ever cognizant of its time and reporting responsibilities.

How deed of trust construed

Every deed of trust to secure debts or indemnify sureties is in the nature of a contract and shall be construed according to its terms to the extent not in conflict with the requirements of law.

Unless otherwise provided therein, it shall be construed to impose and confer upon the parties thereto, and the beneficiaries thereunder, the following duties, rights and obligations in like manner as if the same were expressly provided for by such deed of trust:

1. The deed shall be construed as given to secure the performance of each of the covenants entered into by the grantor as well as the payment of the primary obligation.

2. The grantor shall be deemed to covenant that he will pay all taxes, levies, assessments and charges upon the property, including the fees and charges of

such agents or attorneys as the trustee may deem advisable to employ at any time for the purpose of the trust, so long as any
obligation upon the grantor under the deed of trust remains undischarged.

3. The grantor shall be deemed to covenant that he will keep the improvements on the property in tenantable condition, whether such improvements were on the property when the
deed of trust was given or were thereafter placed thereon.

4. The grantor shall be deemed to covenant that no waste shall be committed or suffered upon the property.

5. The grantor shall be deemed to covenant that in the event of his failure to meet any obligations imposed upon him then the trustee or any beneficiary may, at his option, satisfy the
same. The money so advanced, with interest thereon as provided in the deed of trust, shall be a part of the debt secured by the deed of trust, in the event of sale to be paid next after the expenses of executing the trust, and shall be otherwise recoverable from the grantor as a debt.

In addition, to the extent not otherwise covered, the grantor shall be deemed to covenant that amount advanced or incurred by the trustee or any beneficiary under a deed of trust (i) with respect to an obligation secured by a lien or encumbrance prior to the lien of the deed of trust or
(ii) for the protection of the lien secured by the deed of trust, together with interest as provided in the deed of

trust, shall be a part of the debt secured by the deed of trust, to be paid next after expenses of executing the trust.

6. A covenant to pay interest shall be deemed a covenant to pay interest on the principal balance as such rate may vary or be modified from time to time by the parties under the original instruments or agreements or a written agreement of modification whether or not recorded, and all the interest on the principal secured by the deed of trust shall be on an equal priority with the principal debt secured by the deed of trust, in the event of sale to be paid next after the expenses
of executing the trust.

Any covenant, otherwise authorized by law, that the lender shall be entitled to share in the gross income or the net income, or the gross rent or revenues, or net rents or revenues of the property, or in any portion of the proceeds or appreciation upon sale or appraisal or similar event, shall be
on an equal priority with the principal debt secured by the deed of trust, in the event of sale to be paid next after the expenses of executing the trust, and shall be specified in the recorded deed of trust or other recorded document in order to be notice of record as against subsequent parties.

7. In the event of default in the payment of the debt secured, or any part thereof; at maturity, or in the payment of interest when due, or of the breach of any of the covenants entered into or imposed upon the grantor, then at the request of any beneficiary the trustee shall forthwith declare all the debts and

obligations secured by the deed of trust at once due and payable and may take possession of the property and proceed to sell the same at auction at the premises or
in the front of the circuit court building or at such other place in the city or county in which the property or the greater part thereof lies, or in the corporate limits of any city surrounded by or contiguous to such county, or in the case of annexed land, in the county of which the land was formerly a part, as the trustee may select upon such terms and conditions as the trustee may deem best.

8. If the sale is upon credit terms, the deferred purchase money shall bear interest from the day of sale and shall be secured by a deed of trust upon the property contemporaneous with the trustee's deed to the purchaser.

9. The party secured by the deed of trust, or the holders of greater than fifty percent of the monetary obligations secured thereby, shall have the right and power to appoint a substitute trustee or trustees for any reason and, regardless of whether such right and power is expressly granted in such deed of trust, by executing and acknowledging an instrument designating and appointing a substitute. When the instrument of appointment has been executed, the substitute
trustee or trustees named therein shall be vested with all the powers, rights, authority and duties vested in the trustee or trustees in the original deed of trust. The instrument of appointment shall be recorded in the office of the clerk wherein the original deed of

trust is recorded prior to or at
the time of recordation of any instrument in which a
power, right, authority or duty conferred by the original
deed of trust is exercised.

Notices required before sale by trustee to owners
A. In addition to the advertisement, the trustee or the
party secured shall give written notice of the time,
date and place of any proposed sale in execution of a
deed of trust by personal delivery or by mail to (i) the
present owner of the property to be sold at his last
known address as such
owner and address appear in the records of the party
secured, (ii) any subordinate lien holder who holds a
note against the property secured by a deed of trust
recorded at least thirty days prior to the proposed sale
and whose address is recorded with the deed of trust,
(iii) any
assignee of such a note secured by a deed of trust
provided the assignment and address of assignee are
likewise recorded at least thirty days prior to the
proposed sale, (iv) any condominium unit owners
association which has filed a lien, (v) any property
owners' association which has filed a lien, and (vi) any
proprietary lessees association which has filed a lien.
Written notice shall be given pursuant to clauses (iv),
(v) and (vi), only if the lien is recorded at least thirty
days prior to the proposed sale. Mailing of a copy of
the advertisement or a notice containing the same
information to the owner by certified or registered mail
no less than fourteen days prior to such sale and to
lien holders, the property owners association or
proprietary lessees' association, their assigns and the

condominium unit owners' association, at the address noted in the memorandum of lien, by ordinary mail no less than fourteen days prior to such sale shall be a sufficient compliance with the requirement of notice. The written notice of proposed sale when given as provided herein shall be deemed an effective exercise of any right of acceleration contained in such deed of trust or otherwise possessed by the party secured relative to the indebtedness secured. The inadvertent failure to give notice as required by this subsection shall not impose liability on either the trustee or the secured party.

If a note or other evidence of indebtedness secured by a deed of trust is lost or for any reason cannot be produced and the beneficiary submits to the trustee an affidavit to that effect, the trustee may nonetheless proceed to sale, provided the beneficiary has given written notice to the person required to pay the instrument that the instrument is unavailable and a request for sale will be made of the trustee upon expiration of fourteen days from the date of mailing of the notice. The notice shall be sent by certified mail, return receipt requested, to the last known address of the person required to pay the instrument as reflected in the records of the beneficiary and shall include the name and mailing address of the trustee. The notice shall further advise the person required to pay the instrument that if he believes he may be subject to a claim by a person other than the beneficiary to enforce the instrument he may petition the circuit court of the county or city where the property or some part thereof lies for an order requiring the beneficiary

to provide adequate protection against any such claim. If deemed appropriate by the court, the court may condition
the sale on a finding that the person required to pay the instrument is adequately protected against loss that might occur by reason of a claim by another person to enforce the instrument.

Adequate protection may be provided by any reasonable means. If the trustee proceeds to sale, the fact that the instrument is lost or cannot be produced shall not affect the authority of the trustee to sell or the validity of the sale.
Failure to comply with the requirements of notice contained in this section shall not affect the validity of the sale, and a purchaser for value at such sale shall be under no duty to ascertain whether such notice was validly given.
In the event of postponement of sale, which may be done in the discretion of the trustee, no new or additional notice need be given pursuant to this section.

Advertisement required before sale by trustee
A. Advertisement of sale by a trustee or trustees in execution of a deed of trust shall be in a
newspaper having a general circulation in the city or county wherein the property to be sold, or any portion thereof; lies pursuant to the following provisions:
 1. If the deed of trust itself provides for the number of publications of such newspaper advertisement, which may be done by using the words "advertisement required" or words of like purport followed by the

number agreed upon, then no other or different advertisement shall be
necessary, provided that, if such advertisement be inserted on a weekly basis it shall be published not less than once a week for two weeks and if such advertisement be inserted on a daily basis it shall be published not less than once a day for three days, which may be consecutive days, in the same manner as if the method were set forth in the deed of trust. Should the deed of trust provide for advertising on other than a weekly or daily basis either of the foregoing provisions shall be complied with in addition to those provided in such deed of trust. Notwithstanding the provisions of the deed of trust, the sale shall be held on any day following the day of the last advertisement which is no earlier than eight days following the first advertisement nor more than thirty days following the last advertisement.

2. If the deed of trust does not provide for the number of publications of such newspaper advertisement, the trustee shall advertise once a week for four successive weeks; provided, however, that if the property or some portion thereof is located in a city or in a county immediately contiguous to a city, publication of the advertisement five different days, which may be consecutive days, shall be deemed adequate. The sale shall be held on any day following the day of the last advertisement which is no earlier than eight days following the first advertisement nor more than thirty days following the last advertisement.
B. Such advertisement shall be placed in that section of the newspaper where legal notices appear or

where the type of property being sold is generally advertised for sale.

C. In addition to the advertisement required by subsection A above, the trustee shall give such other further and different advertisement as the deed of trust may require and in addition may give such additional advertisement as he may deem appropriate.

D. In the event of postponement of sale, which postponement shall be at the discretion of the trustee, advertisement of such postponed sale shall be in the same manner as the original advertisement of sale.

E. Failure to comply with the requirements for advertisement contained in this section shall, upon petition, render a sale of the property voidable by the court.

Contents of advertisements of sale

The advertisement of sale under any deed of trust, in addition to such other matters as may be required by such deed of trust or by the trustee, in his discretion, shall set forth a description of the property to be sold, which description need not be as extensive as that contained in the deed of trust, and shall identify the property by street address, if any, or if none, shall give the general location of the property with reference to streets, routes, or known landmarks. Where available, tax map identification may be used but is not required. The advertisement shall also include the time, place and terms of sale and shall give the name or names of the trustee or trustees. It shall
set forth the name, address and telephone number of

such person (either a trustee or the party secured or his agent or attorney) as may be able to respond to inquiries concerning the sale.

Powers and Duties of trustee in event of sale under a deed of trust

A. In the event of sale under a deed of trust, the trustee shall have the following powers and duties in addition to all others:

1. Written one-price bids may be made and shall be received by the trustee from the beneficiary or any other person for entity by announcement of the trustee at the sale. Any person other than the trustee may bid at the foreclosure sale, including a person who has submitted a written one-price bid. Upon request to the trustee or trustees, any other bidder in attendance at a foreclosure sale shall be permitted to inspect written bids. Whenever the written bid of the beneficiary is the highest bid submitted at the sale, such document shall be filed by the trustee with his account of sale. The written bid submitted pursuant to this subsection may be prepared by the beneficiary, its agent or attorney.

2. The trustee may require of any bidder at any sale a cash deposit of as much as ten per centum of the sale price (unless the deed of trust specifies a higher or lower maximum, which may be done by the words "bidder's deposit of not more than... dollars may be required," or words of like purport) before his bid is received, which

shall be returned to the bidder unless the property is sold to him, otherwise to be applied to his credit in settlement or, should he fail to complete his purchase promptly, to be applied to pay the costs and expense of sale and the balance, if any, to be retained by the trustee as his compensation in connection with that sale.

3. The trustee shall receive and receipt for the proceeds of sale, no purchaser being required to see to the application of the proceeds, account for the same to the commissioner of accounts and apply the same, first, to discharge the expenses of executing the trust, including a reasonable commission to the trustee; secondly, to discharge all taxes, levies, and assessment, with costs and interest if they have priority over the lien of the deed of trust, including the due pro rata thereof for the current year; thirdly, to discharge in the order of their priority, if any, the remaining debts and obligations secured by the deed, and any liens of record inferior to the deed of trust under which sale is made, with lawful interest; and, fourthly, the residue of the proceeds shall be paid to the grantor or his assigns; provided, however, that the trustee as to such residue shall not be bound by any inheritance, devise, conveyance, assignment or lien of or upon the grantor's equity, without actual notice thereof prior to distribution; provided further that such order of priorities shall not be changed or varied by the deed of trust.
B. Upon discharge (other than by sale by the trustee) of all debts, duties and obligations imposed by the deed upon the grantor, including any expenses

incurred preparatory to sale,
then upon the grantor's request the trustee shall
execute and deliver a good and sufficient deed of
release at the grantor's own proper costs and
charges.

***Courtesy of National Foreclosure Professionals
and Virginia State Statutes**

Washington*
Washington is a judicial and non-judicial state.
The majority of loans are foreclosed by the non-
judicial method.

Elements of Washington Foreclosures Include:
1 Mailing and posting the Notice of Default out (wait
approximately 30 days).
2 Setting the Trustee's Sale that includes recording
mailing and posting of the Notice of
Trustee's Sale (must be done more than 90 days
before sale date).
3 Publication -2 times at specific intervals in the last
month before sale.
4 Holding the Sale (Must be at least 190 days after
date of first default)
5 Sales can be continued up to 120 days.

Notice of Default
At least 30 days prior to setting a Trustee's Sale, the
beneficiary or trustee must mail a Notice of Default to
the borrower and grantor both by first class and
certified or registered mail, and either post the Notice
of Default on the premises or personally serve the

Notice on the borrower and grantor. The Notice of Default identifies the Deed of Trust and the nature of the default, and gives an itemized account of the arrearage and the foreclosure costs and fees. Loans that are being foreclosed non-judicially may be reinstated any time up through 11 days before the Trustee's Sale. Whether to accept reinstatement after that date is the prerogative of the lender. The loan may be paid off at any time before the sale.

Notice of Trustee's Sale
After 30 days have elapsed from the mailing and posting or serving of the Notice of Default, and at least 90 days prior to the sale, the trustee must mail a Notice of Trustee's Sale to the borrower and grantor and to lien holders, and other parties with an interest in the property who are specified in the Deed of Trust Act.

 1. The Notice of Trustee's Sale must also be recorded with the auditor of the county where the property secured by the Deed of Trust is located, and either posted or personally served more than 90 days before the sale date.

2. The trustee must also mail a Notice of Foreclosure to the grantor with the Notice of Trustee's Sale. Trustee's Sales may only be set in public places on Fridays   between 9:00 a.m. and 4:00 p.m., unless Friday is a legal holiday, in which case, it may be set on the following Monday.

3. The Notice of Trustee's Sale must be published in a legal newspaper at specified times on 2 occasions in the month before the sale. The Trustee's Sale may be continued by the trustee for any cause the trustee deems advantageous, for a period or periods not exceeding 120 days. A Trustee's Sale may be reset for a date no sooner than 45 days after a bankruptcy case is dismissed or closed or relief granted from the automatic stay, if the sale was stayed by the bankruptcy and the time (120 days) has elapsed for continuing the sale. Trustee's Sales are made without warranty as to title, possession, or encumbrances. After the Sale, a Trustee's Deed is recorded reciting that the Sale was conducted in compliance with the Deed of Trust Act. The Act contains special provisions regarding the procedure for restraining a Trustee's Sale.

*Courtesy of National Foreclosure Professionals and Washington State Statutes

West Virginia*
West Virginia is a Judicial State
Requires suit to be filed and service on the debtor, who is then allowed sufficient time to answer the suit according to the procedure and rules. Thereafter, the mortgagee is free to schedule a hearing during which the court will typically enter an order authorizing the sale of the property by a special commissioner appointed by the court.

Notice of Sale

The notice of sale is usually posted on the front door of the courthouse for the county in which the property to be sold is located, and in three (3) other public places, one of which must be the property itself, at least twenty (20) days prior to sale. The notice must also be served upon the borrower and subordinate lien holders at least twenty (20) days prior to the foreclosure sale.

The notice must also contain the time and place of the foreclosure sale, the names of the parties to the deed, the date of the deed, recording information, a property description and the terms of the sale.

The sale must be held at the time and place stated in the foreclosure notice and completed by public auction to the highest bidder. Unless the deed specifies the terms of sale, the buyer must pay one-third (1/3) of the bid amount in cash at the sale.

Deficiency Judgment
Deficiency actions are generally not permitted in West Virginia.

Rights of Redemption
There are no rights of redemption in West Virginia.
*Courtesy of West Virginia State Statutes

Wisconsin*
Wisconsin is a Judicial State
This usually involves filing a lawsuit to obtain a court order to foreclose. Mail the notice of entry of judgment. Verify the period of redemption. File the bill of costs. Set a date for the
Sheriff sale.

Notice of Sale
Publish a notice of the sheriff's sale. It must be published for six full weeks and the last publication must be completed at least one week prior to the day of the sale. The notice must be posted is three public places and contain the sale date, time, and location.

Auction
Once proof is obtained of the posting and publishing of the sale, the auction is held, where the bid must be paid unless it is by the plaintiff and is the amount of the judgment or less. A report is made of the final sale and a motion date is set for confirmation of sale.

The sale must be held at the time and place stated in the foreclosure notice. The winning bidder will receive a certificate of purchase.

Redemption Period
Unless the foreclosure sale has been confirmed by court order, the borrower has one year (12 months) to redeem the property by paying the amount of the highest bid at the foreclosure sale, plus interest.

*Courtesy of Wisconsin State Statutes

Wyoming*
Wyoming is a Judicial State
The process is brought about with a complaint requisition foreclosure of the mortgage and a deficiency judgment on the note. The mortgagor has

20 days to respond to the letter of complaint. Judgment is entered and notice of sale is given along with the time, place, and location of sale. A notice of sale will be published in a local newspaper, after which time the sale will commence.

Sale on foreclosure of mortgage.

When a mortgage is foreclosed a sale of the premises shall be ordered. The decree directing the sale is sufficient warrant for the sheriff or other officer to proceed to advertise and conduct the sale. An order of sale issued by the clerk of court or an appraisement of the real property to be sold is not necessary. When the premises to be sold are in one (1) or more tracts, the court may direct the officer who makes the sale to subdivide and sell the same in parcels, or to sell anyone (1) of the tracts as a whole.

Sale to be at public vendee

No lands or tenements shall be sold by virtue of any execution or decree of foreclosure unless the sale is by public vendee between the hours of 10:00 a.m. and 5:00 p.m. of the same day, nor unless the time and place of holding the sale was previously advertised for four (4) consecutive weeks in the county newspaper in the county where the lands and tenements are situate. The notice shall state the names of the plaintiff and defendant in the action, and the time and place of sale. In all notices the lands or tenements to be sold shall be described with reasonable certainty by appropriate description. If any officer sells any lands or tenements by virtue of any execution or decree, otherwise than as provided, the officer so offending shall forfeit and pay fifty dollars

($50.00) for every offense, to be recovered with costs in any court of record in this state by the person whose lands were advertised and sold.

Certificate of purchase

When real property is sold by virtue of an execution, order of sale, decree of foreclosure or foreclosure by advertisement and sale, the sheriff or other officer, instead of executing a deed to the premises sold, shall give to the purchaser of the lands a certificate in writing describing the property purchased and the sum paid therefore, or if purchased by the plaintiff in execution or by the mortgagee, the amount of his bid. The certificate shall state that the purchaser is entitled to a deed for the property at the expiration of the period of redemption, unless the property is redeemed prior to that date as provided by law. The sheriff or other officer shall record in the office of the recorder of the county a duplicate of the certificate, signed and acknowledged by
him, and the certificate or a certified copy thereof is admissible as evidence of the facts therein contained.

Right of redemption

(a) Except as provided with respect to agricultural real estate, it is lawful for any person, his heirs, executors, administrators, assigns or guarantors whose real property has been sold by virtue of an execution, decree of foreclosure, or foreclosure by advertisement and sale within
three (3) months from the date of sale, to redeem the real estate by paying to the purchaser, his heirs,

executors, administrators or assigns, or to the sheriff or other officer who sold the property, for the benefit of the purchaser, the amount of the purchase price or the amount given or bid if purchased by the execution creditor or by the mortgagee under a mortgage, together with interest at the rate of ten percent (10%) per annum from the date of sale plus the amount of any assessments or taxes and the amount due on any prior lien which the purchaser paid after the purchase, with interest. On payment of this amount the sale and certificate granted are void.

(b) In the case of any mortgage upon one (1) or more parcels of real estate any or all of which were agricultural real estate on the date of execution of the mortgage as stated in the mortgage, the period within which the owner, his heirs, executors, administrators, assigns or guarantors may redeem the premises sold is twelve (12) months from the date of the sale.

(c) The term "agricultural real estate" means any parcel of land in excess of twenty (20) acres lying outside the exterior boundaries of any incorporated city, town or recorded subdivision. If the mortgage recites that the real estate involved is agricultural real estate, it is presumed the parties to the mortgage, their heirs, executors, administrators, assigns, guarantors or successors in interest have agreed to and are bound by all the provisions of law relative to the right of redemption.
*Courtesy of Wyoming State Statutes

About The Co-Authors:

Tim and Julie Harris have been leaders since day one of their careers. After selling more than 100 homes in their very first year and every year thereafter. They gained great acclaim when the National Association or Realtors named them Agents of the Year in 1997. They were consistently rated on the NARs lists of top 500 Agents in the US. They were also the youngest and fastest to achieve the Re/Max Platinum award. They are both Howard Brinton StarPower Stars, and have been long-time coaches for the Mike Ferry Organization. Having been involved in thousands of real estate transactions, Tim and Julie have shown their acumen not just for the business itself, but their abilities to impact their coaching clients.

Tim and Julie Harris are unique in the coaching and training field because they have actually done what they teach. In an industry filled with professional 'speakers' and 'gurus' whom have never sold real estate or haven't sold real estate in decades Tim and Julie stand out - Matter of fact, they are still involved in the real estate sales industry every day.

Tim and Julie have contributed directly to the success of thousands of real estate professionals nationwide, through their unique and proven techniques. With over tens of thousands of coaching calls, they are proud to have some of the most successful agents in the country enrolled at The Harris Real Estate University.

Every day, over 11,000 agents participate in a Harris Real Estate University coaching program.

For more information, find Tim and Julie Harris at:

www.HarrisRealEstateUniversity.com
or
www.TimAndJulieHarris.com

Ronald O Escobar

 Is the Broker Officer for Los Angeles Apartment Corporation and Select Real Estate where he oversees the activities of this high performing team. In addition, Ron is constantly engaged with his personal clients in a wide variety of Real Estate related deals. Ron is a holds the coveted Certified Distressed Property Specialist designation from Harris Real Estate University, where he is an active contributor and the Co-Author and translator of the book "Short Selling Your Home ".

Mr. Escobar is very proud to have served in the Marine Corps as an enlisted Non Commissioned Officer, and later, with the help of the GI Bill putting himself through school and earning a Bachelor Degree in Business, focusing on Sales and Entrepreneurship from the University of Southern California (USC) in 1997. After several years of working, he returned to his alma-mater and earned his MBA with focus Entrepreneurial Finance in 2002. Mr. Escobar is currently attending Concord Law School and is expected to graduate in 2012 with a Jurist Doctorate Degree. Ron holds a California Real Estate Broker license as well as a General Contractor license.

As a former Vice President for Washington Mutual in Century City, CA, he learned the "ins and outs" of mortgage residential and commercial lending. Since then Ron has brokered dozens of millions in mortgages. As a Real Estate broker he has closed over $100 million in transaction value. As a General Contractor he has developed an repositioned a large number of properties. Ron speaks and writes fluently in English and Spanish and is conversational in Portuguese.

www.Select-RealEstate.com
OR
www.ShortSaleCentral.org